Directions (1–50): For each question, write on the answer sheet provided the *number* of the word or expression that, of those given, best completes the statement or answers the question.

1. The geography of the Atlantic Coastal Plain most influenced the southern economy during the period from 1620 to 1865 because it
(1) promoted a plantation system of agriculture
(2) led to diversified manufacturing
(3) encouraged development of the railroad industry
(4) resulted in widespread mining of coal   1 __A__

2. Which event during the Colonial Era most influenced the concept of freedom of the press?
(1) passage of the Navigation Acts
(2) trial of John Peter Zenger
(3) creation of the Albany Plan of Union
(4) establishment of the House of Burgesses   2 ____

3. The social contract theory as applied to the Declaration of Independence most directly reflects the ideas of
(1) John Locke   (3) Baron de Montesquieu
(2) Thomas Hobbes   (4) Adam Smith   3 ____

4. A principal reason for calling the Constitutional Convention of 1787 was to
(1) strengthen the central government
(2) settle land disputes with Canada
(3) increase the power of the states
(4) weaken the system of checks and balances   4 __1__

5. One reason Antifederalist governors of New York and Virginia opposed ratification of the United States Constitution was because it would
(1) force them to abandon western land claims
(2) weaken the powers of state governments
(3) strengthen slavery
(4) make the amendment process more difficult   5 __2__

6. Political parties, the president's cabinet, and national nominating conventions are considered examples of
(1) delegated powers   (3) the elastic clause
(2) separation of powers   (4) the unwritten constitution   6 __1__

7. Thomas Jefferson used a loose interpretation of the United States Constitution when he
(1) negotiated the purchase of the Louisiana Territory from France in 1803
(2) asked Congress to increase the size of the United States Navy
(3) ran for a second term as president
(4) opposed the reelection of John Adams in 1800   7 ___

8. Between 1820 and 1850, Southern lawmakers consistently opposed protective tariffs because these tariffs
(1) decreased trade between the states   (3) increased the cost of imports
(2) harmed American shipping   (4) weakened national security   8 ___

9. In the 1840s, westward expansion was justified by a belief in
(1) laissez-faire   (3) cultural pluralism
(2) popular sovereignty   (4) Manifest Destiny   9 ___

10. Which reform movement is most closely associated with William Lloyd Garrison, Frederick Douglass, and Harriet Beecher Stowe?
(1) abolitionist   (2) labor   (3) Populist   (4) Progressive   10 _1_

Base your answers to questions 11 and 12 on the statements below and on your knowledge of social studies.

Speaker A: The political union created by the Constitution of the United States is not a temporary compact of the states but rather an unbreakable bond created by the people of the nation.

Speaker B: The reserved powers are clearly indicated and protected in both the original Constitution and in the 10th amendment of the Bill of Rights.

Speaker C: Liberty is best preserved in the hands of the government closest to the people. Union is desirable only if it preserves our liberty.

Speaker D: Nullification! Secession! What miserable words-words that threaten the continuance of both our liberty and our Union.

11. Which two speakers express the greatest support for the concept of States rights?
(1) *A* and *B*   (2) *A* and *D*   (3) *B* and *C*   (4) *C* and *D*   11 ___

12. The political opinions expressed in these statements relate most directly to the start of which war?
(1) Revolutionary War   (3) Mexican-American War
(2) War of 1812   (4) Civil War   12 ___

13. Passage of the Kansas-Nebraska Act (1854) was criticized by Northern newspapers because it
(1) limited settlement in those territories
(2) repealed the 36°30′ line of the Missouri Compromise
(3) upheld the Supreme Court decision in *Gibbons* v. *Ogden*
(4) admitted Maine to the Union as a free state   13 ___

U. S. HISTORY — August 2018

14. After the Civil War, the most common occupations for freedmen were
(1) sharecroppers and tenant farmers
(2) factory owners and teachers
(3) skilled artisans and mechanics
(4) miners and soldiers

15. Which geographic factor presented a major problem for settlers on the Great Plains?
(1) limited rainfall
(2) dense forests
(3) mountainous terrain
(4) frequent flooding

Base your answer to question 16 on the graphic organizer and on your knowledge of social studies.

Graphic organizer with central blank and surrounding bubbles: Policy of open immigration; Available natural resources; Abundant food supply; Government policies that support business.

16. Which title is most appropriate for this graphic organizer?
(1) Rise of Labor Unions
(2) Innovations and Technology
(3) Vertical Integration of Business
(4) Factors Contributing to Industrialization

17. In the United States, third parties have been influential because they have often
(1) outspent their political opponents
(2) provided the presidential candidate of the major parties
(3) suggested reforms later adopted by the two major parties
(4) elected majorities in both Congress and state legislatures

18. One purpose of the Chinese Exclusion Act (1882) was to
(1) speed construction of the western railroads
(2) encourage settlement of the Pacific Coast
(3) expand the civil rights of immigrants
(4) protect the jobs of American workers

19. The Interstate Commerce Act of 1887 and the Sherman Antitrust Act of 1890 were passed by Congress to
(1) help regulate the money supply
(2) promote investment in manufacturing
(3) control business practices that limited competition
(4) limit the hours of working women

20. Which demographic change resulted from the economic developments of the late 1800s?
(1) an increase in African American migration from the North to the South
(2) an increase in the number of people living in urban areas
(3) a decrease in the number of immigrants coming to the United States
(4) a decrease in the number of factory workers in the Northeast

21. Between 1900 and 1930, United States relations with Latin America were characterized by repeated United States efforts to
(1) encourage the redistribution of land to the poor
(2) deny economic aid to developing nations
(3) limit the influence of communist dictators
(4) control the internal affairs of many nations in the region

22. President Theodore Roosevelt earned a reputation as a trustbuster because he
(1) favored the conservation of natural resources
(2) used court actions to break up business monopolies
(3) sided with labor unions against big business
(4) opposed the efforts of consumer advocates

23. One way in which Ida Tarbell, Upton Sinclair, and Jacob Riis were similar is that each sought to
(1) end racial discrimination
(2) control illegal immigration
(3) limit government regulations
(4) expose economic and social abuses

24. The purpose of the initiative, referendum, and recall was to
(1) eliminate the two-party system
(2) limit participation in state elections
(3) increase citizen influence in government
(4) strengthen the power of political machines

Base your answer to question 25 on the photograph and on your knowledge of social studies.

Bibb Mill No. 1, Macon, Ga.

Source: Lewis Hine, January 19, 1909

25. Which conclusion is most clearly supported by this photograph?
(1) Textile manufacturing was not important to the national economy.
(2) State and federal governments did not adequately regulate child labor.
(3) American factories were less productive than factories in other countries.
(4) Strict federal safety standards were enforced in factories across the nation.

26. During the 1920s, Congress established a quota system for immigration in order to
(1) ensure that the United States would have enough factory workers
(2) keep migrant workers out of the country
(3) reduce immigration from southern and eastern Europe
(4) assist refugees from war-torn countries

27. Which event is an example of nativism in the 1920s?
(1) the trial of Sacco and Vanzetti
(2) the verdict in the Scopes trial
(3) the Teapot Dome scandal
(4) the stock market crash

28.
- They are suffering because they have little control over the prices for what they produce.
- They have worldwide competition.
- They have difficulty organizing to protect themselves.
- They pay high prices for capital goods.

Which group's economic situation in the 1920s is most accurately described in these statements?
(1) farmers
(2) railroad companies
(3) manufacturers
(4) factory workers

Base your answers to questions 29 and 30 on the cartoon and on your knowledge of social studies.

29. The main idea of this political cartoon from the 1930s is that President Franklin D. Roosevelt
(1) continued the laissez-faire policies of earlier presidents
(2) supported business over labor
(3) favored government ownership of major industries
(4) extended help to those in need

"Yes, You Remembered Me"

Source: C. D. Batchelor, *New York Daily News*, October 11, 1936

30. The New Deal attempted to carry out the theme of the cartoon by
(1) restricting labor union membership
(2) loaning money to foreign countries
(3) funding many public works projects
(4) banning the sale of stocks and bonds

31. The defeat of President Franklin D. Roosevelt's "court packing" plan by Congress is an example of
(1) federalism
(2) checks and balances
(3) due process
(4) the amendment process

Base your answer to question 32 on the excerpt from the letter below and on your knowledge of social studies.

... This new phenomenon [nuclear chain reaction] would also lead to the construction of bombs, and it is conceivable-though much less certain-that extremely powerful bombs of a new type may thus be constructed ....

Yours very truly,
Albert Einstein

—Letter to President Franklin D. Roosevelt from Albert Einstein, August 2, 1939

32. The administration of President Franklin D. Roosevelt reacted to the information contained in this letter by
(1) declaring war on the Axis powers
(2) creating the Manhattan Project
(3) proposing the Lend-Lease plan
(4) initiating the D-Day invasion of Europe

33. The internment of Japanese Americans during World War II primarily affected those Japanese Americans who lived
(1) in the Ohio River valley
(2) along the Gulf Coast
(3) on the West Coast
(4) near the Rio Grande border with Mexico

34. After World War II, one important outcome of the passage of the Servicemen's Readjustment Act of 1944 (GI Bill) was that it
(1) allowed women to serve in combat positions
(2) limited suburban growth
(3) provided funds for new military bases
(4) created educational and housing assistance for veterans

35. What was the primary reason for the creation of both the Truman Doctrine and the Marshall Plan?
(1) to reward the Chinese for their role in the Allied victory over Japan
(2) the fear of Soviet communist expansion throughout Europe
(3) the need to support colonial independence movements in the developing world
(4) the protection of vital United States interests in Middle East oil fields

36. The United States responded to the Berlin blockade in 1948 by
(1) boycotting German-made imports
(2) building the Berlin Wall
(3) stopping all traffic leaving Berlin
(4) airlifting food and supplies into Berlin

37. A major significance of the Korean War (1950-1953) is that for the first time
(1) an atomic bomb was used in warfare
(2) Asian and United States troops fought against each other
(3) the United Nations used military force to oppose aggression
(4) the Soviet Union and the United States supported the same side   37 ___

38. **"All Federal Employees Required to Take Loyalty Oath"**
"Army-McCarthy Hearings Begin"
"Rosenbergs Convicted"
These newspaper headlines from the decade following World War II are all connected to the
(1) war crimes trials in Japan
(2) passage of civil rights legislation in the United States
(3) fear of communism in the United States
(4) debate over economic aid to Europe   38 ___

39. In 1962, President John F. Kennedy responded to the discovery of nuclear missiles in Cuba by
(1) ordering a naval quarantine of Cuba
(2) capturing strategic locations in Cuba
(3) threatening to invade the Soviet Union
(4) prohibiting travel to the southeastern United States   39 ___

40. During the 1960s, the actions of Cesar Chavez led to improved conditions for
(1) coal miners
(2) migrant farm workers
(3) autoworkers
(4) health care workers   40 ___

41. Which phrase best completes the heading of the partial outline below?
    I. Native American Indian _____
       A. Occupation of Alcatraz
       B. Wounded Knee (1973)
       C. Formation of American Indian Movement (AIM)
(1) Support for the War on Poverty
(2) Demands for Equality
(3) Attempts to Culturally Assimilate
(4) Protests Against the Vietnam War   41 ___

42. Which document is the result of President Jimmy Carter's efforts to increase stability in the Middle East?
(1) Camp David Accords
(2) Nuclear Test Ban Treaty
(3) Panama Canal Treaty
(4) Paris Peace Accords   42 ___

43. What was the reason the Equal Rights Amendment did not become part of the United States Constitution?
(1) President Ronald Reagan vetoed it.
(2) Three-fourths of the states did not ratify it.
(3) The National Organization for Women (NOW) did not support it.
(4) The Supreme Court ruled it was unconstitutional.   43 ___

44. Which combination of factors contributed most directly to the severe recession in the United States economy in 2008?
(1) immigration restrictions and lack of skilled workers
(2) cuts in defense spending and social welfare programs
(3) excessive use of credit and bank speculation in the mortgage market
(4) tight monetary policy and overregulation of banks 44 ___

Base your answer to question 45 on the cartoon below and on your knowledge of social studies.

Source: Walt Handelsman, *Newsday*, April 26, 2006

45. The main idea of this cartoon is that public approval of the president in 2006 was directly linked to the
(1) cost of gasoline in the United States
(2) success in stopping human rights abuses abroad
(3) ability to restrict the flow of illegal drugs
(4) amount of the budget surplus 45 ___

Base your answer to question 46 on the cartoon below and on your knowledge of social studies.

Source: Jim Morin, *Miami Herald*, May 10, 2015

46. The main idea of this cartoon is that telephone surveillance by the National Security Administration (NSA)
(1) has been troubled by technical difficulties
(2) violates some of the protections of the United States Constitution
(3) is legal because it protects the privacy of internet users
(4) increases hacking of top-secret government information 46 ___

47. The Alien and Sedition Acts of 1798 were similar to the Espionage and Sedition Acts passed during World War I because they both
(1) provided for the draft of men into the military
(2) gave the government greater control over the production of goods
(3) tried to restrict criticism of and opposition to government policies
(4) attempted to justify United States involvement in a foreign war   47 ___

48. Which set of events in United States history is most closely associated with westward expansion?
(1) passage of the Indian Removal Act of 1830 and the Compromise of 1877
(2) issuing the Emancipation Proclamation of 1863 and creation of the Federal Reserve System in 1913
(3) passage of the Agricultural Adjustment Act of 1933 and creation of the Tennessee Valley Authority in 1933
(4) passage of the Homestead Act of 1862 and opening of the transcontinental railroad in 1869   48 ___

49. The National Association for the Advancement of Colored People (NAACP), the Congress of Racial Equality (CORE), and the Southern Christian Leadership Conference (SCLC) are all associated with which movement?
(1) temperance   (2) abolition   (3) civil rights   (4) environmentalism   49 ___

Base your answer to question 50 on the cartoon and on your knowledge of social studies.

Trying to Close the Gap

Source: Art Bimrose, *Portland Oregonian* (adapted)

50. Which action was an attempt to close the "gap" referred to in the cartoon?
(1) signing the Yalta Agreement
(2) passing the Gulf of Tonkin Resolution
(3) proposing the Strategic Defense Initiative (SDI)
(4) agreeing to the Strategic Arms Limitation Treaty (SALT)   50 ___

PART II
THEMATIC ESSAY QUESTION

Directions: Write a well-organized essay that includes an introduction, several paragraphs addressing the task below, and a conclusion.

Theme: Supreme Court Decisions

> The United States Supreme Court has issued decisions that have defined the constitutional rights of individuals and groups of people. These decisions by the Court have had a great impact on the nation.

Task:

> Select *two* United States Supreme Court cases and for *each*
> - Describe the historical circumstances surrounding the case
> - Explain the Court's decision
> - Discuss the impact of the Court's decision on the United States or on American society

You may use any appropriate Supreme Court case from your study of United States history. Some suggestions you might wish to consider include *Worcester* v. *Georgia* (1832), *Dred Scott* v. *Sanford* (1857), *Plessy* v. *Ferguson* (1896), *Korematsu* v. *United States* (1944), *Brown* v. *Board of Education of Topeka* (1954), *Engel* v. *Vitale* (1962), *Miranda* v. *Arizona* (1966), *Roe* v. *Wade* (1973), and *New Jersey* v. *T.L.O.* (1985).

You are *not* limited to these suggestions.

Guidelines:

In your essay, be sure to:
- Develop all aspects of the task
- Support the theme with relevant facts, examples, and details
- Use a logical and clear plan of organization, including an introduction and a conclusion that are beyond a restatement of the theme

Part III
DOCUMENT-BASED QUESTION

This question is based on the accompanying documents. The question is designed to test your ability to work with historical documents. Some of these documents have been edited for the purposes of this question. As you analyze the documents, take into account the source of each document and any point of view that may be presented in the document. Keep in mind that the language used in a document may reflect the historical context of the time in which it was written.

Historical Context:

> Under the Constitution, Congress has the power to support the armed forces and to declare war, but only the president is authorized to act as commander in chief. Throughout United States history, the president has used his power as commander in chief to respond to many foreign crises. These crises include the ***Mexican-American War (1846-1848)*** during the presidency of James K. Polk, the ***Vietnam War (1964-1975)*** during the presidency of Lyndon B. Johnson, and the ***Persian Gulf War (1990-1991)*** during the presidency of George H. W. Bush.

U. S. HISTORY — August 2018

Task: Using the information from the documents and your knowledge of United States history, answer the questions that follow each document in Part A. Your answers to the questions will help you write the Part B essay in which you will be asked to

Select *two* foreign crises listed in the historical context and for *each*
- Describe the historical circumstances that led to the crisis
- Explain an action taken by the president to respond to the crisis
- Discuss an effect of the president's action on the United States and/or on American society

Part A
Short-Answer Questions

Directions: Analyze the documents and answer the short-answer questions that follow each document in the space provided.

Document 1 United States and Mexico, 1846

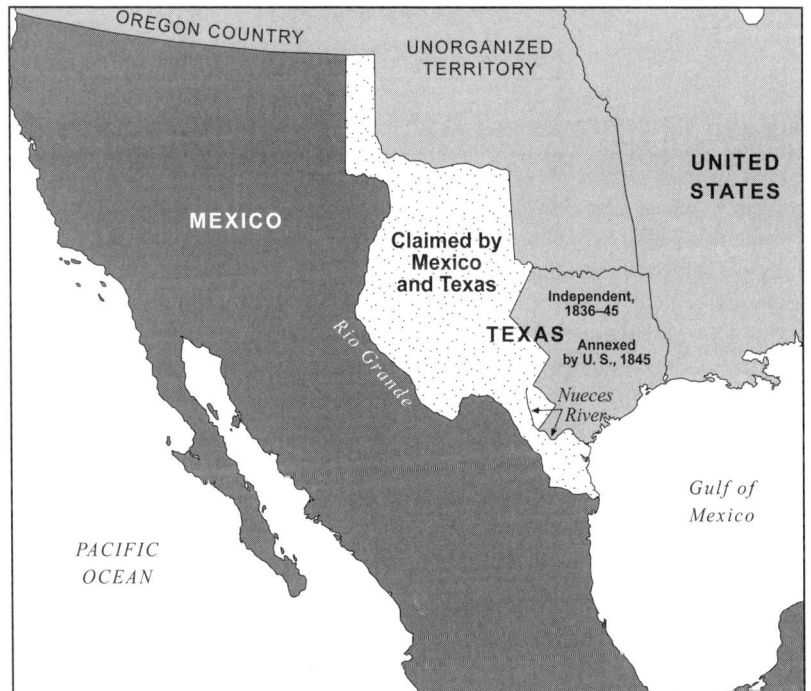

Source: Thomas A. Bailey et al., *The American Pageant*, Houghton Mifflin (adapted)

1. Based on the information provided by this map, state *one* cause of the conflict between the United States and Mexico in 1846. [1]

_____
_____
_____

Document 2

> ... In my message at the commencement of the present session I informed you that upon the earnest appeal both of the Congress and convention of Texas I had ordered an efficient military force to take a position "between the Nueces and the Del Norte [Rio Grande]." This had become necessary to meet a threatened invasion of Texas by the Mexican forces, for which extensive military preparations had been made. The invasion was threatened solely because Texas had determined, in accordance with a solemn resolution of the Congress of the United States [March 1, 1845], to annex herself to our Union, and under these circumstances it was plainly our duty to extend our protection over her citizens and soil. ...

Source: President James K. Polk, War Message, May 11, 1846 (adapted)

2. Based on this document, what action did President James K. Polk take in 1846 regarding Texas? [1]

___

Document 3 **WHY ARE WE IN VIET-NAM?**

> ... Why are these realities our concern? Why are we in South Viet-Nam? We are there because we have a promise to keep. Since 1954 every American President has offered support to the people of South Viet-Nam. We have helped to build, and we have helped to defend. Thus, over many years, we have made a national pledge to help South Viet-Nam defend its independence.
> And I intend to keep that promise.
> To dishonor that pledge, to abandon this small and brave nation to its enemies, and to the terror that must follow, would be an unforgivable wrong.
> We are also there to strengthen world order. Around the globe, from Berlin to Thailand, are people whose well-being rests, in part, on the belief that they can count on us if they are attacked. To leave Viet-Nam to its fate would shake the confidence of all these people in the value of an American commitment and in the value of America's word. The result would be increased unrest and instability, and even wider war ....

Source: "Peace Without Conquest," President Lyndon B. Johnson, Address at Johns Hopkins University, April 7, 1965

3. Based on this document, state *one* reason President Lyndon B. Johnson believed the United States should continue to assist South Vietnam. [1]

Document 4a

> ... It was a peculiarity of nineteenth-century politics that more than a year elapsed between the election of a Congress and its initial meeting. The Thirtieth Congress, elected in 1846, assembled in December 1847 to confront the complex questions arising from the Mexican War. Although Democrats in the Senate outnumbered their opponents by almost two to one, the Whig party enjoyed a narrow margin in the House-the only time in his entire legislative career that Lincoln found himself in the majority. Both parties, however, were internally divided, especially on the question of the future expansion of slavery. In August 1846, just as the previous Congress drew to a close, Congressman David Wilmot of Pennsylvania had proposed an amendment to an appropriation bill requiring that slavery be prohibited in any territory acquired from Mexico. The Wilmot Proviso, which passed the House but failed in the Senate, split both parties along sectional lines and ushered in a new era in which the slavery issue moved to the center stage of American politics ....

Source: Eric Foner, *The Fiery Trial: Abraham Lincoln and American Slavery*, W. W. Norton & Company, 2010

4a. According to Eric Foner, what issue did the Wilmot Proviso attempt to address? [1]

_____

_____

Document 4b   United States Acquisitions from Mexico, 1848

Source: *Historical Maps on File*, Facts on File, 2002 (adapted)

4b. Based on the information provided by this map, what was *one* effect of the Mexican-American War on the United States in 1848? [1]

_____

_____

Document 5a

> ... What are our goals in that war-strained land?
>
> First, we intend to convince the Communists that we cannot be defeated by force of arms or by superior power. They are not easily convinced. In recent months they have greatly increased their fighting forces and their attacks and the number of incidents.
>
> I have asked the Commanding General, General Westmoreland, what more he needs to meet this mounting aggression. He has told me. We will meet his needs.
>
> I have today ordered to Viet-Nam the Air Mobile Division and certain other forces which will raise our fighting strength from 75,000 to 125,000 men almost immediately. Additional forces will be needed later, and they will be sent as requested.
>
> This will make it necessary to increase our active fighting forces by raising the monthly draft call from 17,000 over a period of time to 35,000 per month, and for us to step up our campaign for voluntary enlistments ....

Source: President Lyndon B. Johnson, "Why We Are in Viet-Nam," News Conference, July 28, 1965 (adapted)

5a. Based on this document, what was *one* action President Lyndon B. Johnson took in 1965 regarding Vietnam? [1]

_____

_____

Document 5b   Allied Troop Levels in Vietnam, 1959-1969

Year	United States	South Vietnam	Australia	Korea	New Zealand	Philippines	Thailand
1959	760	243,000	--	--	--	--	--
1960	900	243,000	--	--	--	--	--
1961	3,205	243,000	--	--	--	--	--
1962	11,300	243,000	--	--	--	--	--
1963	16,300	243,000	--	--	--	--	--
1964	23,300	514,000	198	200	30	20	--
1965	184,300	642,500	1,560	20,620	120	70	20
1966	385,300	735,900	4,530	25,570	160	2,060	240
1967	485,600	798,700	6,820	47,830	530	2,020	2,200
1968	536,100	820,000	7,660	50,000	520	1,580	6,000
1969	475,200	897,000	7,670	48,870	550	190	11,570

Source: Church Committee Report on Diem Coup-1963, Vietnam, War Statistics and Facts 1, 25thaviation.org (adapted)

5b. Based on the information in this chart, what was *one* effect of the actions taken by President Lyndon B. Johnson in 1965? [1]

_____

_____

Document 6a

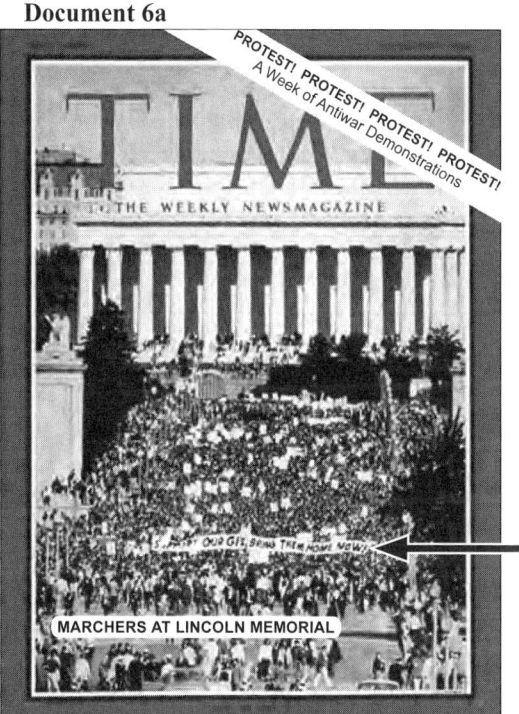

"Support Our GIs, Bring Them Home Now!"

MARCHERS AT LINCOLN MEMORIAL

PROTEST! PROTEST! PROTEST! PROTEST! PROTEST!
A Week of Antiwar Demonstrations

Source: *Time*, October 27, 1967 (adapted)

Document 6b

... With America's sons in the fields far away, with America's future under challenge right here at home, with our hopes and the world's hopes for peace in the balance every day, I do not believe that I should devote an hour or a day of my time to any personal partisan causes or to any duties other than the awesome duties of this office-the Presidency of your country.

Accordingly, I shall not seek, and I will not accept, the nomination of my party for another term as your President. ...

Source: President Lyndon B. Johnson, Address to the Nation Announcing Steps to Limit the War in Vietnam and Reporting His Decision Not to Seek Reelection, March 31, 1968

6. Based on these documents, state *two* effects of the Vietnam War on the United States. [2]

(1) _____

(2) _____

Document 7a

Iraq Deploys Troops Near Kuwait Border Amid Dispute on Oil
WASHINGTON, July 23 -American military officials are closely watching a new deployment of thousands of troops by Iraq along its border with Kuwait, where recent tensions appear to be escalating into a flaunting of strength by the two Persian Gulf countries, Pentagon officials said tonight. ...

Source: *New York Times*, July 24, 1990

Document 7b

**IRAQ ARMY INVADES CAPITAL OF KUWAIT
IN FIERCE FIGHTING
EMERGENCY U.N. SESSION
Casualties Are Called Heavy - Emir's Palace Besieged as Explosions Jolt City**
WASHINGTON, Thursday, August 2 - Iraqi troops crossed the Kuwait border today and penetrated deeply into the country and into Kuwait's capital city, senior Administration officials said late Wednesday ....

Source: *New York Times*, August 2, 1990

Document 7c

Iraq's Naked Aggression
Without warrant or warning, Iraq has struck brutally at tiny Kuwait, a brazen [bold] challenge to world law. Iraq stands condemned by a unanimous U.N. Security Council and major Western oil purchasers. President [George H. W] Bush's taste for bluntness stands him in good stead: "Naked aggression" is the correct term for President Saddam Hussein's grab at a vulnerable, oil-rich neighbor ....

Source: *New York Times*, August 3, 1990

7. Based on these documents, what was *one* cause of the Persian Gulf War? [1]

Document 8

> Just 2 hours ago, allied air forces began an attack on military targets in Iraq and Kuwait. These attacks continue as I speak. Ground forces are not engaged.
>
> This conflict started August 2d [1990] when the dictator of Iraq invaded a small and helpless neighbor. Kuwait-a member of the Arab League and a member of the United Nations was crushed; its people, brutalized. Five months ago, Saddam Hussein started this cruel war against Kuwait. Tonight, the battle has been joined.
>
> This military action, taken in accord with United Nations resolutions and with the consent of the United States Congress, follows months of constant and virtually endless diplomatic activity on the part of the United Nations, the United States, and many, many other countries. Arab leaders sought what became known as an Arab solution, only to conclude that Saddam Hussein was unwilling to leave Kuwait. Others traveled to Baghdad in a variety of efforts to restore peace and justice. Our Secretary of State, James Baker, held an historic meeting in Geneva, only to be totally rebuffed. This past weekend, in a last-ditch effort, the Secretary-General of the United Nations went to the Middle East with peace in his heart-his second such mission. And he came back from Baghdad with no progress at all in getting Saddam Hussein to withdraw from Kuwait.
>
> Now the 28 countries with forces in the Gulf area have exhausted all reasonable efforts to reach a peaceful resolution-have no choice but to drive Saddam from Kuwait by force. We will not fail ....

President George H. W. Bush

Source: President George H. W. Bush, Address to the Nation Announcing Allied Military Action in the Persian Gulf, January 16, 1991

8. Based on this document, what was *one* action taken by President George H. W Bush in response to Iraq's 1990 invasion of Kuwait? [1]

_____
_____
_____

Document 9a

> NEWS of success in the ground war has sent America's hardcore peace activists into retreat and prompted citizens from coast to coast to proclaim that, after two decades, the country is finally purging the "Vietnam syndrome".
>
> While families of servicemen waited anxiously, a sense of pride sometimes approaching glee infused the talk on the streets and on the air waves all day on Sunday and early yesterday. Again and again, people voiced the same view: after all the sneering and humiliation of recent years, America has proved it has the will and the might to fight and win a war ....
>
> Spot opinion polls yesterday showed that well over 80 per cent of the population supported President Bush's decision to launch the ground war, and 75 per cent believed they should keep fighting until President Saddam Hussein is removed.
>
> Commentators and historians are pointing out that Iraq is reaping all the anger pent up through years of humiliation since the debacle and retreat from Vietnam in the early 1970s. USA Today, the popular national newspaper, said the ground war "held the promise of completion, a chance to get past the anguish of Vietnam, and this time to do it right" ....

Source: *The Times*, London, February 26, 1991

Document 9b

> ... Tonight the Kuwaiti flag once again flies above the capital of a free and sovereign nation. And the American flag flies above our Embassy.
>
> Seven months ago, America and the world drew a line in the sand. We declared that the aggression against Kuwait would not stand. And tonight, America and the world have kept their word.
>
> This is not a time of euphoria, certainly not a time to gloat. But it is a time of pride: pride in our troops; pride in the friends who stood with us in the crisis; pride in our nation and the people whose strength and resolve made victory quick, decisive, and just. And soon we will open wide our arms to welcome back home to America our magnificent fighting forces ....

Source: President George H. W. Bush, Address to the Nation on the Suspension of Allied Offensive Combat Operations in the Persian Gulf, February 27, 1991

9. Based on these documents, what were *two* effects of the Persian Gulf War on the United States? [2]

(1) _____

(2) _____

Part B
Essay

Directions: Write a well-organized essay that includes an introduction, several paragraphs, and a conclusion. Use evidence from *at least four* documents in the body of the essay. Support your response with relevant facts, examples, and details. Include additional outside information.

Historical Context:

Under the Constitution, Congress has the power to support the armed forces and to declare war, but only the president is authorized to act as commander in chief. Throughout United States history, the president has used his power as commander in chief to respond to many foreign crises. These crises include the *Mexican-American War (1846-1848)* during the presidency of James K. Polk, the *Vietnam War (1964-1975)* during the presidency of Lyndon B. Johnson, and the *Persian Gulf War (1990-1991)* during the presidency of George H. W. Bush.

Task: Using information from the documents and your knowledge of United States history, write an essay in which you

> Select *two* foreign crises listed in the historical context and for *each*
> - Describe the historical circumstances that led to the crisis
> - Explain an action taken by the president to respond to the crisis
> - Discuss an effect of the president's action on the United States and/or on American society

Guidelines:
In your essay, be sure to
- Develop all aspects of the task
- Incorporate information from *at least four* documents
- Incorporate relevant outside information
- Support the theme with relevant facts, examples, and details
- Use a logical and clear plan of organization, including an introduction and a conclusion that are beyond a restatement of the theme

U. S. HISTORY
January 2019
Part I

Answer all questions in this part.

Directions **(1–50):** For each statement or question, write on the space provided the *number* of the word or expression that, of those given, best completes the statement or answers the question.

1. Which geographic feature was most important for the development of commerce in the New England and middle colonies?
(1) limited rainfall
(2) natural harbors
(3) long growing season
(4) mountainous terrain   1 _____

2. Britain ended the practice of salutary neglect following the French and Indian War (1754-1763) which directly contributed to the
(1) end of the African slave trade
(2) refusal of France to give up Canada
(3) increased conflict with Spain along the Mississippi River
(4) colonial protests of Americans against new taxes   2 _____

3. The Northwest Ordinance (1787) and the Homestead Act (1862) both reflected the national government's policy of
(1) encouraging the settlement of frontier lands
(2) protecting the tribal lands of Native American Indians
(3) expanding slavery onto the Great Plains
(4) purchasing land from foreign countries   3 _____

4. The primary aim of the writers of the United States Constitution was to
(1) eliminate the bicameral legislature
(2) strengthen the power of the central government
(3) preserve the supremacy of the states
(4) weaken the independence of the judiciary   4 _____

Base your answers to questions 5 and 6 on the passage below and on your knowledge of social studies.

... The Executive and the Legislative are so dangerously blended as to give just cause of alarm, and every thing relative thereto, is couched in such ambiguous terms-in such vague and indefinite expression, as is a sufficient ground without any other objection, for the reprobation [disapproval] of a system, that the authors dare not hazard to a clear investigation ....
There is no provision for a rotation, nor any thing to prevent the perpetuity [permanence] of office in the same hands for life; which by a little well timed bribery, will probably be done, to the exclusion of men of the best abilities from their share in the offices of government ....
— Mercy Otis Warren, 1788

5. What reason does Mercy Otis Warren give for the position she stated concerning the executive and legislative branches?
(1) The duties of the president and of Congress were not clearly separated.
(2) Federal courts were a threat to individual liberty.
(3) The thirteen states could never agree on important issues.
(4) The United States Constitution would benefit only a wealthy few.   5 _____

6. Which remedy has been proposed to correct a problem identified by the author concerning elected offices?
(1) campaign spending restrictions
(2) expansion of the civil service system
(3) term limits on members of Congress
(4) direct election of the president   6 _____

Base your answer to question 7 on the map and on your knowledge of social studies.

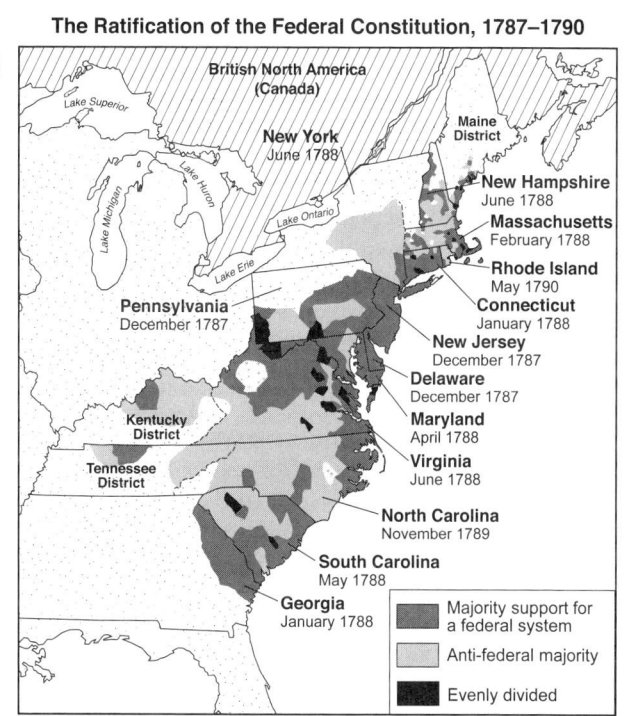

The Ratification of the Federal Constitution, 1787–1790

- New York — June 1788
- Maine District
- New Hampshire — June 1788
- Massachusetts — February 1788
- Rhode Island — May 1790
- Pennsylvania — December 1787
- Connecticut — January 1788
- New Jersey — December 1787
- Delaware — December 1787
- Kentucky District
- Maryland — April 1788
- Tennessee District
- Virginia — June 1788
- North Carolina — November 1789
- South Carolina — May 1788
- Georgia — January 1788

Legend:
- Majority support for a federal system
- Anti-federal majority
- Evenly divided

Source: Martin Gilbert, *Atlas of American History*, Dorset Press, 1985 (adapted)

7. Which area of the United States showed the strongest support for ratification of the Constitution?
(1) coastal areas near the Atlantic Ocean
(2) frontier areas west of the Appalachian Mountains
(3) farming areas in western New York and Pennsylvania
(4) mountain areas in the South   7 _____

8. The power of the president to veto laws and the power of the House of Representatives to impeach are examples of
(1) federalism   (3) executive privilege
(2) the unwritten constitution (4) checks and balances   8 _____

9. As stated in the United States Constitution, which group is directly elected by the people?
(1) Supreme Court justices   (3) members of the House of Representatives
(2) presidential cabinet members   (4) political party leaders   9 _____

Base your answer to question 10 on the table and on your knowledge of social studies.

Number of Electors for Selected States

State	Election of 1904 (476 total)	Election of 2012 (538 total)
New York	39	29
Massachusetts	16	11
Pennsylvania	34	20
Illinois	27	20
Florida	5	29
Texas	18	38
California	10	55

Source: U.S. Electoral College

10. Which trend about the population of the United States is most clearly implied by the information in the table?
(1) States with warmer climates had larger population increases than those in other regions of the United States.
(2) The rural percentage of the population increased throughout the 20th century.
(3) Voter turnout increased in the North and in the East.
(4) Life expectancy increased in the South and in the West, but decreased in other regions. 10 ____

11. Which statement most accurately describes the principle of federalism?
(1) States have the power to review national laws.
(2) The ultimate power is given to the voters.
(3) Power is divided between the national and state governments.
(4) Power is shared by the two political parties. 11 ____

12. The purchase of the Louisiana Territory in 1803 was supported by farmers in Ohio, Kentucky, and Tennessee primarily because they wanted to
(1) end conflicts with Mexico on the western frontier
(2) gain unrestricted access to the Mississippi River and the port of New Orleans
(3) end the practice of slavery
(4) secure an easier route for transporting their products to the Pacific Coast 12 ____

13. The Supreme Court decisions in *McCulloch* v. *Maryland* (1819) and in *Gibbons* v. *Ogden* (1824) resulted in
(1) large land grants for Native American Indians
(2) an expansion of the rights of African Americans
(3) greater state regulation of business activities
(4) an increase in the power of the federal government over state governments 13 ____

14. In the first half of the 19th century, canal building was important to economic growth because canals
(1) could be used in all seasons of the year
(2) provided access to free homesteads in the West
(3) charged lower rates than the transcontinental railroad
(4) allowed faster transport of farm and industrial products 14 ____

U. S. HISTORY — January 2019

15. The victory of Andrew Jackson in the presidential election of 1828 was aided by
(1) the support of eastern bankers
(2) implementing woman's suffrage
(3) reducing property qualifications for voting
(4) the endorsement of northern abolitionists   15 _____

16. Which 19th-century phrase best describes the overall efforts of the United States to expand westward to the Pacific Ocean?
(1) "Remember the Alamo"   (3) "Bleeding Kansas"
(2) "Manifest Destiny"   (4) "Remember the Maine"   16 _____

17. Which action was an attempt by southern state governments after the Civil War to limit the rights of African Americans?
(1) ratification of the 13th amendment
(2) implementation of the Black Codes
(3) establishment of the Freedmen's Bureau
(4) impeachment of President Andrew Johnson   17 _____

18. Political rights for women grew most rapidly on the western frontier primarily because
(1) the settlers were influenced by Native American Indian societies
(2) women greatly outnumbered men in the West
(3) pioneer life often required men and women to share responsibilities equally
(4) immigrants settling in the West brought ideals of gender equality from Europe   18 _____

19. The formation of business monopolies in the late 1800s was made possible by the
(1) effects of laissez-faire policies
(2) passage of federal antitrust laws
(3) elimination of the free-enterprise system
(4) adoption of socialist economic practices   19 _____

20. Which pairing matches a 19th-century business leader with the industry he developed?
(1) Cornelius Vanderbilt-textile   (3) J. P. Morgan-sugar
(2) Andrew Carnegie-meatpacking   (4) John D. Rockefeller-oil   20 _____

21. In the late 1890s, yellow journalism most directly influenced the United States government's decision to
(1) build the Panama Canal
(2) open Japan to trade with the West
(3) enter the Spanish-American War
(4) purchase Alaska and Hawaii   21 _____

22. " ... It is not the mission of the United States to set right everything that is amiss all over the world, even if we have interests involved, or to take part in remodelling the government of some four hundred millions of people who deeply resent foreign interference with their affairs .... " — Josiah Quincy, 1900

The author of this statement is expressing his support for
(1) business investment in foreign countries
(2) war as an instrument of foreign policy
(3) the policy of imperialism
(4) the principle of noninvolvement

23. W E. B. Du Bois and Booker T. Washington strongly disagreed over the
(1) need for passage of the 14th amendment to acquire civil rights
(2) benefits of the Harlem Renaissance
(3) method and speed for attaining equal rights for African Americans
(4) use of the federal policy of affirmative action to aid African Americans

24. Which idea best expresses the philosophy of Progressive reformers?
(1) Economic growth should take priority over social concerns.
(2) Government actions should promote solutions to problems in society.
(3) Reform should come from private business leaders.
(4) Labor unions could undermine the free enterprise system.

"THE IMMIGRANT.
Is he an acquisition or a detriment?"

Source: Victor Gillam, *Judge*, September 19, 1903 (adapted)

25. Which statement most accurately represents the point of view depicted in this 1903 cartoon?
(1) Literacy tests are needed to limit immigration to the United States.
(2) Americans significantly disagree over immigration policy.
(3) The nation's economy depends on continuing large-scale immigration.
(4) Nativist opposition to immigration is declining.

26. As related to Latin America, the Roosevelt Corollary strengthened the original Monroe Doctrine by
(1) threatening military intervention to stop European interference
(2) extending the doctrine to Asia
(3) sending humanitarian aid to Mexico and the Caribbean
(4) promoting the independence of former United States colonies   26 ____

27. Which legislation resulted from the publication of Upton Sinclair's novel, *The Jungle*?
(1) Hepburn Act   (3) Meat Inspection Act
(2) Dawes Act   (4) Interstate Commerce Act   27 ____

28. The main reason the United States Senate did not approve the Treaty of Versailles in 1919 was because the treaty
(1) did not force Germany to return conquered territory
(2) threatened to draw the nation into future international conflicts
(3) failed to include war reparations
(4) was opposed by President Woodrow Wilson   28 ____

29. The Palmer Raids after World War I were controversial because the federal government
(1) led a campaign against discrimination and racial segregation
(2) imprisoned suffragists who led protest marches
(3) violated the civil liberties of suspected radicals
(4) granted asylum to European refugees   29 ____

30. During the 1920s, the influence of the Ku Klux Klan and the passage of laws setting immigration quotas illustrated the
(1) rejection of traditional religious values
(2) support for integrated public schools
(3) negative reaction to the Scopes trial
(4) growth of nativism   30 ____

31. Which factor in the late 1920s was a major cause of the Great Depression?
(1) overproduction of manufactured goods   (3) limited use of consumer credit
(2) high income tax rates   (4) low tariffs on European products   31 ____

32. What was one reason many banks failed during the early 1930s?
(1) Banks had made risky loans and stock market investments.
(2) Banks were overregulated by the federal government.
(3) Large banks had formed a monopoly.
(4) Banks charged high interest rates for loans.   32 ____

33. One major policy difference between President Herbert Hoover and President Franklin D. Roosevelt was that President Roosevelt
(1) focused primarily on reducing tariffs
(2) stressed tax cuts and subsidies for big business
(3) adopted a laissez-faire philosophy
(4) proposed direct aid to farmers and the unemployed   33 ____

34. President Franklin D. Roosevelt's first 100 days are regarded by many historians as successful because
(1) the Senate agreed to join the League of Nations
(2) he increased the number of Supreme Court Justices
(3) many of his New Deal proposals were enacted into law
(4) the Great Depression came to an end   34____

35. Which heading would be most accurate for the partial outline below?

I. _____
   A. United States restricts arms sales in 1935.
   B. President Roosevelt gives "quarantine" speech in 1937.
   C. Cash-and-carry policy goes into effect in 1939.
   D. Britain receives lend-lease aid in 1941.

(1) Congress Expands War Powers
(2) Media Influences Foreign Policy
(3) United States Moves Away From Neutrality
(4) International Community Unites for Peace   35____

36. After the attack on Pearl Harbor, President Franklin D. Roosevelt decided to
(1) ban Japanese Americans from serving in Congress
(2) deport most Japanese Americans to Japan
(3) immediately draft all young Japanese Americans into the military
(4) move Japanese Americans to internment camps away from the Pacific Coast   36____

37. Agreements made at the Yalta and Potsdam conferences near the end of World War II resulted in the
(1) division of Germany into zones of occupation
(2) invasion of the Soviet Union by the Allies
(3) creation of the arms control agreements
(4) control of the Korean peninsula by United Nations forces   37____

Base your answers to questions 38 and 39 on the cartoon and on your knowledge of social studies.

Source: Fred O. Seibel, *Richmond Times-Dispatch*, March 14, 1947 (adapted)

38. The point of view expressed by this cartoonist is that this "new" United States foreign policy is
(1) risky and may not succeed
(3) a violation of the United Nations Charter
(2) certain to lead to another war
(4) too expensive to support   38____

39. Which United States foreign policy is being referred to in this cartoon?
(1) Neutrality Act
(2) Atlantic Charter
(3) Truman Doctrine
(4) Manhattan Project   39 ____

Base your answer to question 40 on the passage below and on your knowledge of social studies.

... You have to take chances for peace, just as you must take chances in war. Some say that we were brought to the verge of war. Of course we were brought to the verge of war. The ability to get to the verge without getting into the war is the necessary art. If you cannot master it, you inevitably get into war. If you try to run away from it, if you are scared to go to the brink, you are lost ....
— Secretary of State John Foster Dulles, *Time*, January 23, 1956

40. The policy described by Secretary Dulles was most evident in the later actions of the United States during the
(1) Cuban missile crisis
(2) Nuclear Test Ban Treaty
(3) energy crisis of 1973
(4) Camp David talks between Egypt and Israel   40 ____

41. Which social change was accelerated by the passage of the Interstate Highway Act in 1956?
(1) revitalization of urban areas
(2) demand for new forms of public transportation
(3) growth of the Northeast's population relative to that of the South and West
(4) movement from cities to new suburban communities   41 ____

42. United States involvement in Vietnam in the early 1960s was justified by a widely held belief that
(1) United States economic prosperity depended on taking control of South Vietnam
(2) failure to defend freedom in South Vietnam would result in communist domination of Southeast Asia
(3) supporting South Vietnam would honor United States obligations to the North Atlantic Treaty Organization (NATO)
(4) involvement in Southeast Asia was necessary to prevent communists from seizing control of China   42 ____

43. • October 4, 1957-Soviet Union launches *Sputnik*
    • April 12, 1961-a Soviet cosmonaut is the first person to orbit Earth
    • February 20, 1962-John Glenn is the first American to orbit Earth
    • July 20, 1969-Neil Armstrong walks on the Moon

Which conclusion do these events directly support?
(1) The United States was the first to orbit Earth.
(2) The United States space program eventually surpassed the Soviet Union's program.
(3) The Soviet Union and the United States both militarized space.
(4) *Sputnik* had little domestic influence on the United States.   43 ____

44. Since the 1960s, a major goal of the women's movement has been to gain
(1) full property rights
(2) better access to public education
(3) equal economic opportunity
(4) the right to vote   44 ____

45. The main argument used by President Richard Nixon to block publication of the *Pentagon Papers* was that their disclosure would
(1) damage his environmental policies
(2) jeopardize trade relationships
(3) harm the prosperity of the nation
(4) threaten national security   45 ____

Base your answer to question 46 on the excerpt below and on your knowledge of social studies.

... Question: Mr. President, many people in Congress believe in the tax cuts—I mean, the budget cuts, but are very concerned about the tax cuts. They fear it will be inflationary. How do you plan to combat that fear among Congress?

President Reagan: Well, I mentioned that last night, this fear that the tax cuts would be inflationary. First of all, a number of fine economists like Murray Weidenbaum and many of his associates don't think that that's so. But also we've got history on our side. Every major tax cut that has been made in this century in our country has resulted in even the government getting more revenue than it did before, because the base of the economy is so broadened by doing it ....
— Question-and-Answer Session with President Ronald Reagan, 1981

46. Based on this excerpt, President Ronald Reagan's economic policy called for
(1) reducing taxes to increase investment by private businesses
(2) increasing government spending on social welfare programs
(3) limiting military spending to balance the federal budget
(4) raising taxes to decrease inflation   46 ____

47. The USA Patriot Act (2001) was passed to
(1) recruit volunteers for military service
(2) protect the United States from terrorists
(3) prohibit citizens from criticizing government policies
(4) safeguard civil liberties from abuse by the government   47 ____

Base your answer to question 48 on the cartoon below and on your knowledge of social studies.

Source: Mike Keefe, *Denver Post*, March 16, 2011

48. Which statement most accurately expresses the main idea of this cartoon?
(1) Nuclear power plants are subject to risks.
(2) Nuclear waste should not be dumped into the oceans.
(3) The government should encourage the construction of nuclear facilities.
(4) Nuclear power plants are the targets of terrorists. 48 ___

49. • Pure Food and Drug Act passed.
    • Graduated income tax established.
    • Federal Reserve System created.

These events occurred during which historic period?
(1) Reconstruction   (3) Roaring Twenties
(2) Progressive Era   (4) Cold War   49 ___

50. One way in which the Square Deal, the New Frontier, and the Great Society are similar is that each was a
(1) plan to promote big business
(2) campaign to extend woman's suffrage
(3) book written by a muckraking journalist
(4) presidential program of reform   50 ___

Part II
THEMATIC ESSAY QUESTION

Directions: Write a well-organized essay that includes an Introduction, several paragraphs addressing the task below, and a conclusion.

Theme: Government Actions

> Throughout United States history, the federal government has taken actions that have either expanded or limited the rights of individuals in the United States. These government actions have had significant political, social, and economic impacts on the nation.

Task: Choose *two* federal government actions that have expanded or limited the rights of individuals and for *each*

- Describe the historical circumstances that led to the government action
- Discuss the impact of the action on the United States and/or American society

You may use any government action that expanded or limited the rights of individuals from your study of United States history. Some suggestions you might wish to consider include the Indian Removal Act (1830), *Dred Scott* v. *Sanford* (1857), the 15th amendment (suffrage for African American males, 1870), *Plessy* v. *Ferguson* (1896), *Schenck* v. *United States* (1919), the 18th amendment (Prohibition, 1919), the 19th amendment (woman's suffrage, 1920), *Brown* v. *Board of Education of Topeka* (1954), the Civil Rights Act (1964), the Voting Rights Act (1965), and the 26th amendment (suffrage for 18-year-old citizens, 1971).

You are *not* limited to these suggestions.

Guidelines:

In your essay, be sure to:
- Develop all aspects of the task
- Support the theme with relevant facts, examples, and details
- Use a logical and clear plan of organization, including an introduction and a conclusion that are beyond a restatement of the theme

Part III
DOCUMENT-BASED QUESTION

This question is based on the accompanying documents. The question is designed to test your ability to work with historical documents. Some of these documents have been edited for the purposes of this question. As you analyze the documents, take into account the source of each document and any point of view that may be presented in the document. Keep in mind that the language used in a document may reflect the historical context of the time in which it was written.

Historical Context:

Until the mid-1800s, the United States remained a primarily rural, agricultural nation. However, by the early 20th century, the United States had become an urban, industrialized nation. This transition led to problems related to *housing* and *working* conditions. Governments, groups, and individuals have attempted to improve *housing* and *working* conditions with varying degrees of success.

Task: Using information from the documents and your knowledge of United States history, answer the questions that follow each document in Part A. Your answers to the questions will help you write the Part B essay in which you will be asked to

- Describe *housing* conditions and *working* conditions in urban areas during the late 1800s and early 1900s
- Discuss the extent to which efforts to address *housing* and/or *working* conditions were successful

U. S. HISTORY — January 2019

Part A — Short-Answer Questions

Directions: **Analyze the documents and answer the short-answer questions that follow each document in the space provided.**

Document 1

... So many people in so little space: eight hundred per acre in some city blocks. Flies were fat and brazen and everywhere, because in summer the windows and doors had to be open all the time in hopes that a breeze might find its way down the river and through the crowded streets and among the close-packed tenements and across the back of one's neck. Along with the flies came the noise of steel wagon wheels on paving stones, the wails of babies, peddlers bellowing, the roar of elevated trains, hollering children, and the scritch-scratch and tinkle of windup phonographs.

Late summer was a season of dust and grime. Half the metropolis, it seemed, was under construction, a new tower of ten or more stories topping out every five days, competing skyscrapers racing toward the clouds, a third and then a fourth bridge stretching across the East River (where a generation earlier there had been none). The hot, damp air was full of dirt, cement powder, sawdust, and exhaust from the steam shovels ....

Source: David Von Drehle, *Triangle: The Fire that Changed America*, Grove Press, 2003

1. According to David Von Drehle, what were *two* conditions faced by people living in urban areas in the early 1900s? [2]

(1) _____

(2) _____

Document 2

... The razing [tearing down] of the worst tenements through such urban renewal programs and the enactment of stricter regulatory laws are generally credited with bringing an end to the privations [hardships] of the tenement system. From 1867 to 1901, New York enacted a series of increasingly stringent [strict] tenement laws that mandated better ventilation and sanitation, improved maintenance, and indoor plumbing. But to what extent did regulation really contribute to the demise of the tenement menace? Despite the stipulations that each room have a window and that stairwells have better lighting, stench continued to overpower tenement residents, and the promised improvements in ventilation never materialized. Lewis Hinc's photographs from the years after the enactment of the 1901 legislation reveal crowding just as awful as Jacob Riis had found in the late 1880s and nearly as bad as that which antebellum [pre-Civil War] investigators had uncovered in Cow Bay and the Old Brewery [neighborhoods] ....

Source: Tyler Anbinder, *Five Points*, The Free Press, 2001 (adapted)

2. According to Tyler Anbinder, what was *one* attempt to address issues faced by people living in tenements? [1]

_____

_____

Document 3a Family in Room in Tenement House, 1890

Source: Jacob Riis, *How the Other Half Lives: Studies Among the Tenements of New York*, Dover Publications, 1971

Document 3b

Women and Children Working at Home in New York City, early 1900s

Source: Lewis Wickes Hine, December 1911, Library of Congress

3. Based on these photographs, what was *one* condition faced by families living in tenements? [1]

_____

_____

U. S. HISTORY — January 2019   33

Document 4

... As an example to the city, Addams installed a small incinerator at Hull-House and had the settlement house's Woman's Club investigate garbage conditions in the ward and report their findings to city hall. But to no avail. Finally, in desperation, Addams applied to become the Nineteenth Ward's garbage collector. Her bid was never considered, but the publicity it provoked led the city to appoint her the ward's inspector of garbage.

Every morning at 6:00 A.M., neighbors trudging to work would see a bent woman as pale as candle wax following the city's garbage wagons to the dump to see that they did their work thoroughly; and in the evenings Jane Addams would supervise the burning of mountains of alley refuse, the hundred-foot-high flames drawing crowds of curious onlookers. The foreign-born women of the neighborhood were "shocked," Addams recalled, "by this abrupt departure into the ways of men." But some of them came to understand "that their housewifely duties logically extended to the adjacent alleys and streets" where diseases spread by filth put their children at deadly risk.

The unflagging pressure of Addams and other settlement workers-most prominently Mary McDowell in Packingtown-forced the city to take measures to improve sanitary conditions in some immigrant wards. But not until after 1900, and not very satisfactorily ....

Source: Donald L. Miller, *City of the Century: The Epic of Chicago and the Making of America*,
Simon & Schuster, 1996

4. According to Donald L. Miller, what was *one* way settlement workers attempted to improve sanitary conditions in Chicago? [1]

_____

_____

Document 5

... Information collected by the Commission and staff was compiled into several reports, including the two main reports, "The Fire Hazard in Factory Buildings" and "Sanitation of Factories", published in the Preliminary Report of the Factory Investigating Commission (1912). To improve sanitary conditions, the Commission's report to the Legislature recommended registration of all factories with the Department of Labor, licensing of all food manufacturers, medical examinations of food workers, medical supervision in dangerous trades, and better eating, washing, and toilet facilities. To lessen the fire hazard, the Commission recommended an increase in stairwells and exits, installation of fire walls, fireproof construction, prohibition of smoking in factories, fire extinguishers, alarm systems, and automatic sprinklers. The Commission's other reports summarized investigations of and made recommendations concerning women factory workers, child labor in tenements, and occupational diseases such as lead and arsenic poisoning ....

Source: Working Lives: *A Guide to the Records of the New York State Factory Investigating Commision*, New York State Archives and Records Administration, 1989

5. Based on this New York State document, state *one* recommendation made by the Factory Investigating Commission in 1912 to address problems faced by workers. [1] _____

_____

Document 6

On Friday evening, March 24, two young sisters walked down the stairways from the ninth floor where they were employed and joined the horde of workers that nightly surges homeward into New York's East Side. Since eight o'clock they had been bending over shirt-waists of silk and lace, tensely guiding the valuable fabrics through their swift machines, with hundreds of power driven machines whirring madly about them; and now the two were very weary, and were filled with that despondency [hopelessness J which comes after a day of exhausting routine, when the next day, and the next week, and the next year, hold promise of nothing better than just this same monotonous strain ....

"It's worse than it was before the strike, a year ago," bitterly said Gussie, the older [sister]. "The boss squeezes [puts pressure on] us at every point, and drives us to the limit. He carries us up in elevators of mornings [every morning], so we won't lose a second in getting started; but at night, when we're tired and the boss has got all out of us he wants for the day, he makes us walk down. At eight o'clock he shuts the doors, so that if you come even a minute late you can't get in till noon, and so lose half a day; he does that to make sure that every person gets there on time or ahead of time. He 6.nes us for every little thing; he always holds back a week's wages to be sure that he can be able to collect for damages he says we do, and to keep us from leaving; and every evening he searches our pocketbooks and bags to see that we don't carry any goods or trimmings away. Oh, you would think you are in Russia again!" ...

Source: Miriam Finn Scott, "The Factory Girl's Danger," *The Outlook*, April 15, 1911

6. According to Miriam Finn Scott, what were *two* conditions that made factory work difficult in 1911? [2]

_____

_____

Document 7

... In every industry the story was monotonously the same: paupers' wages; the constant fear of dismissal; wretched and unsanitruyworking conditions; ten-, twelve-, and even fourteen-hour days (sixteen for bakers); six- and sometimes seven-day weeks; erratic pay; little or no compensation for injuries or fatalities; a constant increase in the number of women and children employed under such conditions; and, worst of all, the widespread conviction that workingmen and women (not to mention children) had been losing ground ever since the end of the Civil War.

Under such circumstances it is hardly surprising that the number of strikes increased year by year following the Great Strikes of 1877. In 1881 there were 471 strikes affecting 2,928 companies and 129,521 employees. Five years later the number of strikes had risen to 1,411, involving 9,861 companies and almost half a million employees. Roughly half (46 percent) of the struck companies acquiesced in [agreed to] the principal demands of the strikers. Over 3,000 more strikes were partially successful, and 40 percent of the strikes, involving 50 percent of the strikers, were judged "failures." ...

Source: Page Smith, "How the Other Side Lived," *A People's History of the Past, Reconstruction Era, Vol. VI, The Rise of Industrial America*, 1984

continued on next page

7a. According to Page Smith, what was *one* condition faced by industrial workers in the late 1800s? [1]

7b. According to Page Smith, what was *one* attempt made by workers to improve working conditions? [1]

Document 8

... The supreme duty of the Nation is the conservation of human resources through an enlightened measure of social and industrial justice. We pledge ourselves to work unceasingly in State and Nation for:

Effective legislation looking to the prevention of industrial accidents, occupational diseases, overwork, involuntary unemployment, and other injurious effects incident to modem industry;

The fixing of minimum safety and health standards for the various occupations, and the exercise of the public authority of State and Nation, including the Federal control over inter-State commerce and the taxing power, to maintain such standards;

The prohibition of child labor;

Minimum wage standards for working women, to provide a living scale in all industrial occupations;

The prohibition of night work for women and the establishment of an eight hour day for women and young persons;

One day's rest in seven for all wage-workers; ...

We favor the organization of the workers, men and women as a means of protecting their interests and of promoting their progress ....

Source: Platform of the Progressive Party, August 7, 1912

8. Based on this document, what were *two* proposals made in the 1912 Progressive Party Platform that addressed issues faced by workers? [2]

(1)

(2)

Document 9

... Abandoning efforts to secure business cooperation, in 1935 the New Deal moved in the direction of strengthening workers' ability to bargain collectively and effectively, presuming this would lead to fair wages, hours, and working conditions. Competition, together with fair treatment of workers, would keep business functioning properly in an open market. The National Labor Relations Act, proposed by New York senator Robert Wagner and endorsed by FDR [Franklin Delano Roosevelt] once it passed the Senate, had a dramatic effect on many workers. The Wagner Act, as it was frequently called, compelled employers to deal with labor unions that employees-in elections supervised by the National Labor Relations Board (NLRB)-chose to represent them. The act also prohibited unfair labor practices such as discharging workers for union membership, favoring an employer-dominated company union, or refusing to negotiate in good faith with a union. All these practices had long been common before the National Industrial Recovery Act and continued after its adoption. But now, with an independent federal agency overseeing labor-management relations, the weight of the federal government stood behind organized workers in their efforts to negotiate better terms of employment. ....

Source: David E. Kyvig, *Daily Life in the United States, 1920-1940*, Ivan R. Dee, 2002

9. According to David E. Kyvig, state *one* way New Deal programs addressed problems faced by workers. [1]

_____

_____

Part B — Essay

Directions: Write a well-organized essay that includes an introduction, several paragraphs, and a conclusion. Use evidence from *at least five* documents in the body of the essay. Support your response with relevant facts, examples, and details. Include additional outside information.

Historical Context:

Until the mid-1800s, the United States remained a primarily rural, agricultural nation. However, by the early 20th century, the United States had become an urban, industrialized nation. This transition led to problems related to *housing* and *working* conditions. Governments, groups, and individuals have attempted to improve *housing* and *working* conditions with varying degrees of success.

Task: Using information from the documents and your knowledge of United States history, write an essay in which you

- Describe *housing* conditions and *working* conditions in urban areas during the late 1800s and early 1900s
- Discuss the extent to which efforts to address *housing* and/or *working* conditions were successful

Guidelines: In your essay, be sure to
- Develop all aspects of the task
- Incorporate information from *at least five* documents
- Incorporate relevant outside information
- Support the theme with relevant facts, examples, and details
- Use a logical and clear plan of organization, including an introduction and a conclusion that are beyond a restatement of the theme

U. S. HISTORY

June 2019
Part I

Answer all questions in this part.

Directions (1–50): For each statement or question, write on the space provided the *number* of the word or expression that, of those given, best completes the statement or answers the question.

1. In colonial America, the Magna Carta, the English Bill of Rights, and the writings of John Locke contributed to the
(1) diversity of religious beliefs among the colonists
(2) political ideals and practices of the colonists
(3) economic relationships between the colonists and the mother country
(4) demands of colonists to end the slave trade and the practice of slavery   1 ____

2. Before 1763, most American colonists settled near the Atlantic Coast or rivers because
(1) port cities could be more easily defended in times of war
(2) valleys were less fertile
(3) English colonists were only allowed to settle in these locations
(4) navigable water offered easier access to trade and employment   2 ____

3. One way in which the Declaration of Independence and the original United States Constitution are similar is that both promote the idea of
(1) the consent of the governed   (3) voting rights for all adult citizens
(2) equal rights for women   (4) judicial review of unjust laws   3 ____

4. The main purpose of the *Federalist Papers* was to
(1) discourage the creation of political parties
(2) support the candidacy of George Washington
(3) urge ratification of the Constitution
(4) advocate independence from Great Britain   4 ____

5. "... Constitutions should consist only of general provisions: The reason is, that they must necessarily be permanent, and that they cannot calculate for the possible changes of things...."
— Alexander Hamilton, 1788

Which provision of the United States Constitution best supports the idea expressed in this quotation?
(1) eminent domain   (3) separation of powers
(2) electoral college   (4) elastic clause   5 ____

6. The main objection to the adoption of the United States Constitution was based primarily on the belief that
(1) the number of new states admitted to the Union should be limited
(2) individual freedoms could be restricted by a strong central government
(3) a separate judiciary would make the government ineffective
(4) slave populations gave the South too much power   6 ____

7. Which viewpoint of the framers of the United States Constitution is demonstrated by the use of the electoral college to select the president?
(1) distrust of the average citizen's judgment
(2) belief that political parties strengthen the campaign process
(3) desire to end property qualifications for voting
(4) commitment to universal suffrage   7 ____

Base your answer to question 8 on the diagram below and on your knowledge of social studies.

```
                    The legislatures                              The legislatures
                    of three-quarters      NATIONAL               of three-quarters of
THE CONGRESS        of all the states      CONVENTION             all the states
By favorable vote                          Called by Congress
of two-thirds       or                     when requested by      or
of those voting                            two-thirds of the
in both houses      Special state          state legislatures     Special state
                    conventions in                                conventions in
                    three-quarters of                             three-quarters of
                    all the states                                all the states
```
Source: National Archives (adapted)

8. What is the best title for this diagram?
(1) Methods of Amending the Constitution
(2) Procedures of the Executive Branch
(3) Process of Nominating Presidential Candidates
(4) Admission of New States to the Union   8 ____

9. The United States wanted to acquire New Orleans in 1803 in order to
(1) end British influence in North America
(2) promote the growth of manufacturing in the region
(3) establish a military base to defend against attacks from Mexico
(4) secure a port that would improve the transportation of agricultural goods   9 ____

10. The Supreme Court decision in *Gibbons* v. *Ogden* (1824) is important because it
(1) banned the importation of manufactured goods
(2) encouraged state investment in internal improvements
(3) expanded federal control over interstate commerce
(4) permitted taxes on exported goods   10 ____

11. Under Chief Justice John Marshall (1801–1835), Supreme Court decisions generally upheld Alexander Hamilton's belief that
(1) a national debt would violate the economic principles of the Constitution
(2) states should have more economic power than the federal government
(3) the power of Congress should be greater than the power of the president
(4) a loose interpretation of the Constitution could be used to increase federal power   11 ____

Base your answer to question 12 on the passage below and on your knowledge of social studies.

... I am not a Know-Nothing. That is certain. How could I be? How can any one who abhors the oppression of negroes [African Americans], be in favor of degrading classes of white people? Our progress in degeneracy appears to me to be pretty rapid. As a nation, we began by declaring that "*all men are created equal.*" We now practically read it "all men are created equal, *except negroes.*" When the Know-Nothings get control, it will read "all men are created equal, except negroes, *and foreigners, and catholics.*" When it comes to this I should prefer emigrating to some country where they make no pretence of loving liberty —to Russia, for instance, where despotism can be taken pure, and without the base alloy of hypocracy. . . .

— Abraham Lincoln, letter to Joshua Speed, August 24, 1855

12. In this 1855 letter, Abraham Lincoln opposed the Know-Nothing party because it
(1) supported the policy of imperialism
(2) favored unrestricted immigration
(3) promoted resentment against minority groups
(4) wanted equal rights for all people   12 ___

13. The Supreme Court's decision in *Dred Scott* v. *Sanford* was nullified by the passage of the
(1) Kansas-Nebraska Act   (3) Compromise of 1850
(2) 13th and 14th amendments   (4) Reconstruction Act   13 ___

14. The Civil War directly affected the Northern economy by
(1) causing a severe depression
(2) destroying much of its farmland
(3) greatly expanding the canal system
(4) stimulating the growth of factories   14 ___

15. Rapid industrialization during the late 1800s contributed to
(1) a decline in the membership of the American Federation of Labor (AFL)
(2) a reduction in government regulation of railroads
(3) a rise in the number of family farms
(4) an increase in immigration to the United States   15 ___

16. Which factor aided the building of transcontinental railroads?
(1) The federal government provided free land to the railroad companies.
(2) The railroads established fair rates for customers.
(3) Congress repealed antitrust laws against the railroads.
(4) The Supreme Court approved public ownership of the railroad industry.   16 ___

17. Which tactics were used by big business during the late 1800s to limit the power of labor unions?
(1) strikebreakers and lockouts   (3) collective bargaining and mediation
(2) picketing and walkouts   (4) wage increases and shorter hours   17 ___

18. Which constitutional right was the central focus in *Plessy v. Ferguson* (1896)?
(1) freedom of assembly guaranteed by the first amendment
(2) due process of the law in the fifth amendment
(3) equal protection of the law under the 14th amendment
(4) equal voting rights guaranteed by the 15th amendment   18 ___

Base your answer to question 19 on the cartoon and on your knowledge of social studies.

The Monster Monopoly

19. What is being criticized in this cartoon?
(1) environmental damage
(2) business consolidation
(3) oil exploration
(4) federal tax laws

Source: Frank Beard, Judge, July 19, 1884 (adapted)

19 ___

20. Which event was a result of the Spanish-American War?
(1) Cuba was divided into spheres of influence.
(2) Puerto Rico became a possession of the United States.
(3) The Philippines became a Spanish colony.
(4) The United States lost control of the Panama Canal.   20 ___

21. • Chinese Exclusion Act (1882)
    • Gentlemen's Agreement (1907)
    • Emergency Quota Act (1921)

These federal actions demonstrate that Americans have
(1) supported the principle of open immigration
(2) provided immigrants equal access to jobs and social programs
(3) forced immigrants to settle in designated areas
(4) favored limiting immigration at different times in the nation's history   21 ___

22. In the early 20th century, muckraking authors Upton Sinclair and Ida Tarbell primarily criticized the federal government for
(1) wasting money on foreign wars
(2) ignoring abuses committed by big business
(3) excessive regulation of the steel industry
(4) overspending on social welfare programs   22 ___

U. S. HISTORY — June 2019

23. During the Progressive Era, voters were given more opportunities to select political party candidates through
(1) direct primary elections
(2) term limits on elected officials
(3) initiative and recall
(4) public funding of elections   23 ___

24. Theodore Roosevelt's Square Deal and Woodrow Wilson's New Freedom shared the goal of
(1) achieving equal rights for minority groups
(2) protecting the interests of big business
(3) strengthening federal regulatory power over large corporations
(4) instituting laissez-faire policies   24 ___

25. The Federal Reserve System was created in 1913 to
(1) balance the budget
(2) control the money supply
(3) insure savings account deposits
(4) regulate the stock market   25 ___

Base your answer to question 26 on these statements by President Woodrow Wilson and on your knowledge of social studies.

". . . The United States must be neutral in fact as well as in name. . ."
— message to U.S. Senate, 1914

". . . America can not be an ostrich with its head in the sand. . . ."
— address in Des Moines, Iowa, 1916

". . . The world must be made safe for democracy. . . ."
— address to Congress asking for a declaration of war, April 2, 1917

26. What do these statements demonstrate about President Wilson during the three years before the United States entered World War I?
(1) He gradually changed his foreign policy goals.
(2) He eagerly became involved in a war.
(3) He abused the principle of separation of powers.
(4) He was consistent in his policy of strict neutrality.   26 ___

27. President Warren Harding's call for a "return to normalcy" meant the United States should
(1) limit the number of exports
(2) reduce its role in world affairs
(3) expand efforts to end racial discrimination
(4) support woman's suffrage   27 ___

28. Which heading best completes the partial outline below?

I. _____
  A. Overproduction
  B. Underconsumption
  C. Buying on margin
  D. Unequal distribution of wealth

(1) Causes of the Industrial Revolution
(2) Causes of World War I
(3) Causes of the Great Depression
(4) Causes of World War II   28 ___

Base your answer to question 29 on the graph and on your knowledge of social studies.

United States Unemployment Rate, 1927–1939

Source: *Historical Statistics of the United States, Colonial Times to 1970* (adapted)

29. Which conclusion is most clearly supported by the information provided on the graph?
(1) Deficit spending ended unemployment.
(2) World War II increased unemployment.
(3) New Deal programs only partially relieved unemployment.
(4) Unemployment after the New Deal was the same as before the stock market crash.   29 ___

30. During the 1930s, poor land management and severe drought conditions across parts of the Midwest resulted in the
(1) establishment of the United States Department of Agriculture
(2) creation of wheat surpluses
(3) decreased support for conservation
(4) development of the Dust Bowl conditions on the Great Plains   30 ___

31. During the 1930s, United States neutrality legislation was primarily designed to
(1) provide military and economic aid to Italy and Japan
(2) give the United States time to plan an attack against Germany
(3) protect American lives and property in Latin America
(4) avoid foreign policy mistakes that led to involvement in World War I   31 ___

Base your answers to questions 32 and 33 on the song lyrics below and on your knowledge of social studies.

That's Why We're Voting For Roosevelt

Herbie Hoover promised us "Two chickens in each pot,"
Breadlines and Depression were the only things we got.
I lost my job, my bank blew up, and I was on the spot.
That's why I'm voting for Roosevelt.

Hooray! Hooray! Herb Hoover's gone away,
Hooray! Hooray! I hope he's gone to stay.
For now I'm back to work and get my three squares ev'ry day.
That's why I'm voting for Roosevelt. . . .

Wall Street sure is kicking for they know they're on the pan.
Franklin D. in Washington upset their little plan,
And now the one on top is that poor once forgotten man,
That's why we're voting for Roosevelt.

Hooray! Hooray! He banished all our fear.
Hooray! Hooray! Our banks are in the clear.
He brought us back prosperity, he gave us back our beer,
That's why I'm voting for Roosevelt.

— Thomas O'Dowd, 1936

32. Which group would most likely have agreed with the lyrics of this song?
(1) Prohibition advocates
(2) Republican Party leaders
(3) New Deal supporters
(4) Supply-side economists   32 ___

33. According to the song lyrics, people supported Franklin D. Roosevelt primarily because he
(1) implemented economic relief and recovery programs
(2) favored a national suffrage amendment
(3) continued Herbert Hoover's economic policies
(4) reduced federal income taxes   33 ___

Base your answer to question 34 on the cartoon and on your knowledge of social studies.

Source: Vaughn Shoemaker, *Chicago News*, April 27, 1937 (adapted)

34. This cartoon is critical of President Franklin D. Roosevelt's efforts to
(1) force Congress to reduce government waste
(2) convince the Supreme Court to pass a constitutional amendment to balance the budget
(3) reverse the effects of the Great Depression
(4) increase his power over the Supreme Court   34 ___

Base your answers to questions 35 and 36 on the poster and on your knowledge of social studies.

35. The poster indicates that rationing during World War II was a
(1) policy to encourage small-business owners
(2) way of assuring that only the wealthy could buy certain products
(3) necessity caused by farm failures during the Great Depression
(4) program that was to be applied equally to all Americans

Source: Office of Price Administration, 1943

35 ___

36. What was a major reason for wartime rationing?
(1) ensuring that troops were adequately supplied
(2) restricting lower-priced food imports
(3) providing jobs for the unemployed
(4) preventing currency deflation

36 ___

37. What would be the most appropriate heading for the partial outline below?

> I. _____
>   A. Treatment of Japanese Americans
>   B. Segregation of African Americans in the armed forces
>   C. United States reactions to the Nazi Holocaust
>   D. Use of the atomic bomb

(1) Issues of Morality during World War II
(2) Domestic Policies during World War II
(3) Economic Problems during World War II
(4) Reasons for the Success of the Allies during World War II

37 ___

Base your answer to question 38 on the graph and on your knowledge of social studies.

38. What is the title for this graph for the years 1946–1964?
(1) The Graying of America
(2) The Growth of the Middle Class
(3) The Baby Boom Generation
(4) From Suburbs to Cities

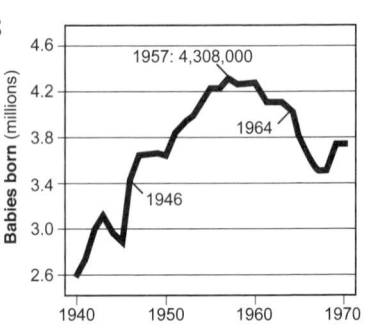

Source: The NYSTROM Atlas of United States History, 2000 (adapted)

38 ___

Base your answers to questions 39 and 40 on the map and on your knowledge of social studies.

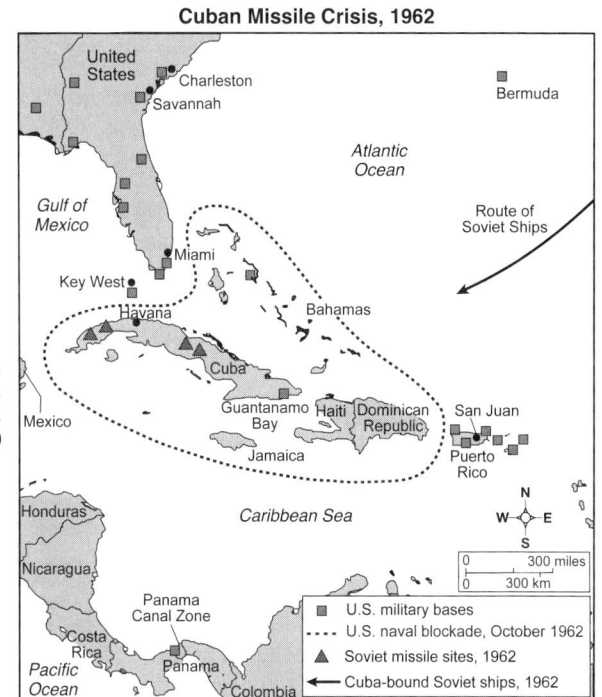

Cuban Missile Crisis, 1962

Source: Gary B. Nash and Carter Smith, *Atlas of American History*, Facts on File, 2007 (adapted)

39. What was the immediate cause of the action taken by the United States that is shown on the map?
(1) Cuban refugees lobbied President Dwight Eisenhower to overthrow Fidel Castro.
(2) The Soviet Union built nuclear missile launch sites within range of United States cities.
(3) United States military bases in the Caribbean were closed by Cuban armed forces.
(4) Puerto Rican citizens asked Congress to assist them in repelling communist advances. 39 ___

40. One positive outcome of the situation shown on the map was that the United States and Soviet Union increased
(1) communication between the two nations to avert war
(2) military control of their Latin American colonies
(3) cooperative humanitarian efforts in Caribbean nations suffering from natural disasters
(4) joint efforts to end the cruel practices of Cuba's leaders 40 ___

41. The main reason President John F. Kennedy proposed the establishment of the Peace Corps was to
(1) promote trade with Africa
(2) combat drug use in American cities
(3) gain support from immigrant voters
(4) improve conditions in developing nations 41 ___

42. What was an outcome of the Watergate affair during the administration of President Richard Nixon?
(1) Presidential powers were expanded.
(2) Respect for the office of the president declined.
(3) The Supreme Court cleared President Nixon of all charges.
(4) Congress refused to take action against President Nixon. 42 ___

43. The goal of the War Powers Act of 1973 was to
(1) allow the president to declare war without congressional approval
(2) give Congress the sole power to authorize the use of military force
(3) limit the president's power to use military force without congressional approval
(4) require a declaration of war for all uses of military forces 43 ___

44. ". . . The United States, together with the United Nations, exhausted every means at our disposal to bring this crisis to a peaceful end. However, Saddam [Hussein] clearly felt that by stalling and threatening and defying the United Nations, he could weaken the forces arrayed against him. . . ."
— President George H. W. Bush, address to the nation, January 16, 1991

President George H. W. Bush used this statement to defend
(1) taking military action to liberate Kuwait from Iraqi aggression
(2) providing foreign aid to Israel
(3) supporting Egypt against attacks by terrorists
(4) using United States troops as peacekeepers in Bosnia 44 ___

Base your answer to question 45 on the cartoon and on your knowledge of social studies.

Source: John de Rosier, *Albany Times Union*, July 29, 2010

45. Which combination of factors has led to the problem shown in the cartoon?
(1) lower medical costs and high interest rates
(2) business monopolies and depletion of natural resources
(3) consumer debt and nearly stagnant wages
(4) population migration and the graying of America 45 ___

46. One way in which the goals of the Know-Nothing Party in the 1850s and the response to the Red Scare of 1919 were similar is that both
(1) called for equal rights for women and African Americans
(2) sought to limit immigration to the United States
(3) supported the overseas expansion of the United States
(4) attempted to limit the influence of big business on American politics 46 ___

47. Which term most accurately describes United States foreign policy during the Cold War?
(1) containment (2) nonalignment (3) Big Stick (4) Open Door 47 ___

Base your answer to question 48 on the chart below and on your knowledge of social studies.

Action	Reaction
President Andrew Johnson disobeys the Tenure of Office Act. →	Congress impeaches Johnson and he remains in office by one vote.
Congress passes the National Industrial Recovery Act (NIRA). →	The Supreme Court declares the NIRA unconstitutional in *Schechter Poultry Corporation v. United States*.

48. Which aspect of governmental power is best illustrated by both examples in the chart?
(1) federalism
(2) checks and balances
(3) States rights
(4) judicial review

49. Which economic policy argues that government should limit, as much as possible, any interference in the economy?
(1) socialism
(2) laissez-faire
(3) mercantilism
(4) protectionism

50. W. E. B. Du Bois, Jackie Robinson, and James Meredith are considered pioneers in the area of
(1) labor relations
(2) educational reform
(3) civil rights
(4) environmental protection

Part II
THEMATIC ESSAY QUESTION

Directions: **Write a well-organized essay that includes an introduction, several paragraphs addressing the task below, and a conclusion.**

Theme: Westward Movement of the Frontier

> Throughout United States history, efforts to settle new land pushed the frontier further west. Several important events influenced this westward movement. These events often led to conflict with Native American Indians or with foreign governments.

Task:

> Select *two* events that significantly influenced the westward movement of the frontier and for *each*
> - Describe the historical circumstances surrounding the event
> - Discuss the positive *and/or* negative effects of the event on the settlement of the West

You may use any event that significantly influenced the westward movement of the frontier from your study of United States history. Some events you might wish to consider include:

> Signing of the Treaty of Paris (1783)
> Creation of the reservation system (1800s)
> Purchase of the Louisiana Territory (1803)
> Opening of the Erie Canal (1825)
> War with Mexico (1846–1848)
> Discovery of gold in California (1848)
> Passage of the Homestead Act (1862)
> Purchase of Alaska (1867)
> Completion of the transcontinental railroad (1869)

You are *not* limited to these suggestions.

Guidelines:

In your essay, be sure to:
- Develop all aspects of the task
- Discuss *at least two* effects for each event
- Support the theme with relevant facts, examples, and details
- Use a logical and clear plan of organization, including an introduction and a conclusion that are beyond a restatement of the theme

Part III
DOCUMENT-BASED QUESTION

This question is based on the accompanying documents. The question is designed to test your ability to work with historical documents. Some of these documents have been edited for the purposes of this question. As you analyze the documents, take into account the source of each document and any point of view that may be presented in the document. Keep in mind that the language and images used in a document may reflect the historical context of the time in which it was created.

Historical Context:

In the decades following World War II, significant domestic and foreign policy issues led to political and social tensions in the United States. These issues motivated individuals and groups to organize protest movements to bring about change. Protest movements such as the *civil rights movement*, the *anti–Vietnam War movement*, and the *environmental movement* met with varying degrees of success.

Task: Using information from the documents and your knowledge of United States history, answer the questions that follow each document in Part A. Your answers to the questions will help you write the Part B essay in which you will be asked to

> Choose *two* protest movements mentioned in the historical context and for *each*
> - Describe the historical circumstances surrounding the protest movement
> - Discuss the extent to which the protest movement was successful

U. S. HISTORY — June 2019

Part A
Short-Answer Questions

Directions: **Analyze the documents and answer the short-answer questions that follow each document in the space provided.**

Document 1a

"AND REMEMBER, NOTHING CAN BE ACCOMPLISHED BY TAKING TO THE STREETS"

Source: Herblock, *Washington Post*, September 6, 1963 (adapted)

Document 1b

If You Miss Me At the Back of the Bus

If you miss me at the back of the bus
you can't find me nowhere
come on over to the front of the bus
I'll be riding up there. . . .

If you miss me on the picket line
you can't find me nowhere
come on over to the city jail
I'll be rooming over there. . . .

If you miss me in the cotton fields
you can't find me nowhere
come on over to the courthouse
I'll be voting right there. . . .

Source: recorded by Pete Seeger, 1963, written by Carver Neblett

1. Based on these documents, state *one* form of discrimination African Americans experienced in the 1960s. [1]

_____
_____
_____

Document 2

> . . . In its regional breadth, the uprising resembled the sit-in movement of 1960. But the 1963 demonstrations [after Birmingham] were more widespread, involved much larger numbers, and drew in people of all ages and backgrounds. To list the places where black people engaged in nonviolent protests would be to name virtually every town and city in the South: about 115 communities experienced 930 demonstrations of one kind or another. The number of people arrested topped 20,000, four times as many as in 1960.
>
> The 1963 surge of nonviolent direct action made the maintenance of segregation in public accommodations untenable [unable to continue]. Black people knew that if segregation could be cracked in Birmingham, it could be cracked anywhere. Birmingham exposed the vulnerability of the South's political regime, and black people seized the opportunity to attack it. In city after city, under the relentless pressure of demonstrations, whites sat down to negotiate. During a single three-week period after Birmingham, the Justice Department noted that 143 cities had acceded [agreed] to some degree of integration. By year's end the number exceeded three hundred. Many cities set up biracial committees that enabled blacks to press for further desegregation. . . .

Source: Adam Fairclough, *Better Day Coming: Blacks and Equality, 1890–2000*, Viking Penguin, 2001

2. According to Adam Fairclough, what was *one* effect of the 1963 demonstrations in Birmingham, Alabama? [1]

_____

_____

Document 3

> American protest against the war in Vietnam was begun and sustained by American citizens who believed that in a representative democracy, individuals can make themselves heard and, more, can affect public policy.
>
> To us, the antiwar movement during the Vietnam era is important not because it stopped the war, which it may or may not have done; rather, it is important because it existed. It is a reminder to Americans that times come when citizens can and, indeed, must challenge their government's authority. . . .
>
> Every war has had its opponents. There was a sizable antiwar sentiment in Great Britain during the South African War (1899–1902), and in America there has always been during every war a small protest movement—most notably, until Vietnam, during the Mexican War in 1846–48 and the Philippine Insurrection in 1899–1901. But the Vietnam War was different: increasingly unpopular, undeclared and therefore in the opinion of many citizens illegal and unconstitutional as well, it was the most frustrating war in American history, and the ugliest, and the longest. The movement opposing it had years in which to grow. . . .

Source: Nancy Zaroulis and Gerald Sullivan, *Who Spoke Up?: American Protest Against the War In Vietnam, 1963–1975*, Holt, Rinehart and Winston, 1984

3. According to Nancy Zaroulis and Gerald Sullivan, what was *one* reason for protest against the Vietnam War? [1]

_____

_____

Document 4

... In far too many ways American Negroes have been another nation: deprived of freedom, crippled by hatred, the doors of opportunity closed to hope.

In our time change has come to this Nation, too. The American Negro, acting with impressive restraint, has peacefully protested and marched, entered the courtrooms and the seats of government, demanding a justice that has long been denied. The voice of the Negro was the call to action. But it is a tribute to America that, once aroused, the courts and the Congress, the President and most of the people, have been the allies of progress.

Thus we have seen the high court of the country declare that discrimination based on race was repugnant [disagreeable] to the Constitution, and therefore void. We have seen in 1957, and 1960, and again in 1964, the first civil rights legislation in this Nation in almost an entire century. . . .

The voting rights bill will be* the latest, and among the most important, in a long series of victories. But this victory—as Winston Churchill said of another triumph for freedom—"is not the end. It is not even the beginning of the end. But it is, perhaps, the end of the beginning."

That beginning is freedom; and the barriers to that freedom are tumbling down. Freedom is the right to share, share fully and equally, in American society—to vote, to hold a job, to enter a public place, to go to school. It is the right to be treated in every part of our national life as a person equal in dignity and promise to all others.

But freedom is not enough. You do not wipe away the scars of centuries by saying: Now you are free to go where you want, and do as you desire, and choose the leaders you please. . . .

This is the next and the more profound stage of the battle for civil rights. We seek not just freedom but opportunity. We seek not just legal equity but human ability, not just equality as a right and a theory but equality as a fact and equality as a result.

For the task is to give 20 million Negroes the same chance as every other American to learn and grow, to work and share in society, to develop their abilities—physical, mental and spiritual, and to pursue their individual happiness. . . .

Source: Lyndon B. Johnson, Commencement Address at Howard University, June 4, 1965

*The Voting Rights Act was signed into law on August 6, 1965.

4a. According to President Lyndon B. Johnson, what is *one* achievement of the civil rights movement? [1]

_____

_____

4b. According to President Lyndon B. Johnson, what is *one* remaining goal for the civil rights movement? [1]

_____

_____

Document 5

...As the U.S. commitment increased, so did the number of bombs dropped on the North, the volume of North Vietnamese coming into the South, the fervor of the protest movement, the billion dollar military grants, and the number of casualties. Johnson's pledge to fight communism in Southeast Asia had degenerated into what anti-war folk singer Pete Seeger labeled "the Big Muddy." And yet, the refrain of that song said, "the old fool says to push on." Tempers on both sides flared as the body counts increased, and each night's TV broadcasts introduced American viewers to faraway hell holes where their sons, brothers, friends, and husbands were stepping on land mines, perishing in Vietcong mantraps, and being cut down in hand-to-hand combat. The week of September 18–24 brought with it a grim statistic: 142 U.S. soldiers killed, 825 wounded, 3 missing—the war's highest toll in 1966....

Every time American troops won a small victory or held a strategic position, the President's advisers used the occasion to press for more troops and more money. These were vital, they repeatedly declared, to consolidate our gains and increase our advantages. The monthly draft was doubled several times, up to 46,000 a month in October 1966, as General Westmoreland constantly increased his call for troops. He had almost a half-million men in combat by April 1967. By the following year, he told the President, he would need almost 700,000. With that number, he said, we could win the war in two years. The "light at the end of the tunnel," which President Johnson optimistically referred to in his news broadcasts, had dimmed considerably since his earlier predictions....

Source: Toby Goldstein, *Waking from the Dream: America in the Sixties*, Julian Messner, 1988

5. According to Toby Goldstein, what were *two* reasons for the development of the anti–Vietnam War movement? [2]

(1)_____

(2)_____

Document 6a

Millions Join Earth Day Observances Across the Nation

Throngs jamming Fifth Avenue yesterday in response to a call for the regeneration of a polluted environment.

Source: *New York Times*, April 23, 1970 (adapted)

Document 6b

Earth Day, the first mass consideration of the globe's environmental problems, preempted [commanded] the attention and energies of millions of Americans, young and old, across the country yesterday. . . .

Organizers of Earth Day said more than 2,000 colleges, 10,000 grammar and high schools, and citizen groups in 2,000 communities had indicated intentions of participating. . . .

The purpose of the observance was to heighten public awareness of pollution and other ecological problems, which many scientists say urgently require action if the earth is to remain habitable. . . .

Summarizing the implications of the day's activities, Senator Nelson said: "The question now is whether we are willing to make the commitment for a sustained national drive to solve our environmental problems." . . .

Source: Gladwin Hill, "Activity Ranges From Oratory to Legislation," *New York Times*, April 23, 1970

6. Based on these documents, state *one* reason the observance of Earth Day is important to the environmental movement. [1]

Document 7

. . . For the first time in the history of the world, every human being is now subjected to contact with dangerous chemicals, from the moment of conception until death. In the less than two decades of their use, the synthetic pesticides have been so thoroughly distributed throughout the animate and inanimate world that they occur virtually everywhere. They have been recovered from most of the major river systems and even from streams of groundwater flowing unseen through the earth. Residues of these chemicals linger in soil to which they may have been applied a dozen years before. They have entered and lodged in the bodies of fish, birds, reptiles, and domestic and wild animals so universally that scientists carrying on animal experiments find it almost impossible to locate subjects free from such contamination. They have been found in fish in remote mountain lakes, in earthworms burrowing in soil, in the eggs of birds—and in man himself. For these chemicals are now stored in the bodies of the vast majority of human beings, regardless of age. They occur in the mother's milk, and probably in the tissues of the unborn child. . . .

Source: Rachel Carson, *Silent Spring*, Houghton Mifflin, 1962

7. According to Rachel Carson, what is *one* issue that has led to concerns about the environment? [1]

Document 8

... The impact of the antiwar protests remains one of the most controversial issues raised by the war. The obvious manifestations [displays] of dissent in the United States probably encouraged Hanoi's will to hold out for victory, although there is nothing to suggest that the North Vietnamese would have been more compromising in the absence of the movement. Antiwar protest did not turn the American people against the war, as some critics have argued. The effectiveness of the movement was limited by the divisions within its own ranks. Public opinion polls make abundantly clear, moreover, that a majority of Americans found the antiwar movement, particularly its radical and "hippie" elements, more obnoxious than the war itself. In a perverse sort of way, the protest may even have strengthened support for a war that was not in itself popular. The impact of the movement was much more limited and subtle. It forced Vietnam onto the public consciousness and challenged the rationale of the war and indeed of a generation of Cold War foreign policies. It limited Johnson's military options and may have headed off any tendency toward more drastic escalation. Perhaps most important, the disturbances and divisions set off by the antiwar movement caused fatigue and anxiety among the policymakers and the public, and thus eventually encouraged efforts to find a way out of the war. ...

Source: George C. Herring, *America's Longest War: The United States and Vietnam, 1950–1975*, Alfred A. Knopf, 1986 (adapted)

8*a*. According to George C. Herring, what was *one* way the anti–Vietnam War movement was *not* successful? [1]

8*b*. According to George C. Herring, what was *one* way the anti–Vietnam War movement was successful? [1]

Document 9a

... Earth Day had consequences: it led to the Clean Air Act of 1970, the Clean Water Act of 1972, and the Endangered Species Act of 1973, and to the creation, just eight months after the event, of the Environmental Protection Agency. Throughout the nineteen-seventies, mostly during the Republican Administrations of Richard Nixon and Gerald Ford, Congress passed one environmental bill after another, establishing national controls on air and water pollution. And most of the familiar big green groups are, in their current form, offspring of Earth Day. Dozens of colleges and universities instituted environmental-studies programs, and even many small newspapers created full-time environmental beats. ...

Source: Nicholas Lemann, "When the Earth Moved: What Happened to the Environmental Movement?" *The New Yorker*, April 15, 2013

9a. According to Nicholas Lemann, what is *one* impact of Earth Day? [1]

Document 9b

Frances Beinecke served as president of the Natural Resources Defense Council [NRDC] from 2006–2014. The Council writes and lobbies for public policy to protect the environment.

My work at NRDC has brought me to the front lines of the climate crisis. I have flown over the massive tar sands strip mines in the boreal forest. I have visited the homes of people coping with frack pads [an area of land used in the fracking process] and wastewater ponds in their backyards. And I have helped my neighbors recover from the devastation of Superstorm Sandy. ...

Never in my lifetime have the challenges been greater than those we face from climate change. Never have the solutions been more clearly at hand. We know how to defuse the climate threat. We just have to act now. ...

It's time for us, as Americans, to state as a national goal that we'll hit fast-forward on efforts to clean up our carbon pollution, invest in energy efficiency and shift to renewable power so that we will become a carbon-neutral nation that no longer contributes to climate change. ...

We have already begun slashing climate change pollution. More than 3.4 million Americans are on the job every day helping to clean up our dirty power plants, get more electricity from the wind and sun, manufacture more hybrid and electric cars, and cut energy waste in our homes, at work and on the road. ...

The modern environmental movement exists for one purpose: we're here to change the world—to become a place where we care for the natural systems of the Earth as if our very lives depended on them, because they do. That is not yet the world we live in. It is the world we must create.

Source: Frances Beinecke, "The World We Create: My New Book and a Message of Hope for the Planet," *Switchboard: National Resources Defense Council Blog*, October 14, 2014

9b. According to Frances Beinecke, state *one* reason the environmental movement continues to be important. [1]

Part B
Essay

Directions: Write a well-organized essay that includes an introduction, several paragraphs, and a conclusion. Use evidence from **at least four** documents in the body of the essay. Support your response with relevant facts, examples, and details. Include additional outside information.

Historical Context:

> In the decades following World War II, significant domestic and foreign policy issues led to political and social tensions in the United States. These issues motivated individuals and groups to organize protest movements to bring about change. Protest movements such as the *civil rights movement,* the *anti–Vietnam War movement,* and the *environmental movement* met with varying degrees of success.

Task: Using information from the documents and your knowledge of United States history, write an essay in which you

> Choose *two* protest movements mentioned in the historical context and for *each*
> • Describe the historical circumstances surrounding the protest movement
> • Discuss the extent to which the protest movement was successful

Guidelines:

In your essay, be sure to
- Develop all aspects of the task
- Incorporate information from *at least four* documents
- Incorporate relevant outside information
- Support the theme with relevant facts, examples, and details
- Use a logical and clear plan of organization, including an introduction and a conclusion that are beyond a restatement of the theme

U. S. HISTORY

August 2019
Part I

Answer all questions in this part.

Directions (1–50): For each statement or question, write on the space provided the *number* of the word or expression that, of those given, best completes the statement or answers the question.

1. Which geographic features contributed to the economic development of the plantation system in the South?
(1) rocky soil and deep harbors
(2) short rivers and many waterfalls
(3) rich soil and warm climate
(4) high mountains and numerous rivers   1 _____

2. The slogan "no taxation without representation" was first used by Americans to protest Britain's
(1) policy of salutary neglect
(2) issuance of the Proclamation of 1763
(3) passage of the Coercive Acts
(4) attempts to raise revenue through the Stamp Act   2 _____

3. Weaknesses in the central government under the Articles of Confederation exposed by Shays' Rebellion contributed directly to the
(1) signing of the Declaration of Independence
(2) creation of the United States Constitution
(3) development of a policy of neutrality
(4) passage of the Northwest Ordinance   3 _____

4. A central issue in the debate between Federalists and Antifederalists over the ratification of the United States Constitution was the
(1) power of judicial review being granted to the judicial branch
(2) threat posed by a strong central government to the rights of citizens
(3) role of the president as commander in chief of the armed forces
(4) danger of unrestricted interstate commerce   4 _____

5. During the 1790s, which factor best explains why the United States was able to stay out of foreign conflicts?
(1) Europe depended on farm products from the United States.
(2) The United States had announced the Monroe Doctrine.
(3) France and Great Britain agreed to end colonialism.
(4) The Atlantic Ocean helped the United States remain isolated from foreign threats.   5 _____

6. Which statement describes an effect of the Louisiana Purchase (1803)?
(1) The size of the United States was doubled.
(2) The boundary with Mexico was finally established.
(3) The Northwest Territory became part of the United States.
(4) The Mississippi River became the western boundary of the United States.   6 _____

7. Many New England citizens opposed United States participation in the War of 1812 because they
(1) feared a Russian invasion in the Northwest
(2) worried that France might try to regain Canada
(3) resented disruption of their trade with England
(4) resisted the extension of slavery into western territories 7 ___

8. The protection against double jeopardy and the right to a speedy trial are evidence that the United States Constitution supports the principle of
(1) eminent domain   (3) representative democracy
(2) due process of law   (4) reserved powers 8 ___

9. During the early 1800s, advances in democratic government included
(1) eliminating property ownership as a voting requirement
(2) ending the role of the electoral college
(3) increasing education and religious requirements for voting
(4) giving states the right to secede from the Union 9 ___

10. One reason abolitionists were unpopular with many Northerners from the 1830s to 1860 was because the abolitionists
(1) favored the growth of slavery
(2) encouraged the annexation of Texas
(3) advocated views that increased tensions with the South
(4) supported the Fugitive Slave Law 10 ___

11. The Compromise of 1850 was an attempt to resolve issues related to
(1) the protection and spread of slavery
(2) boundary disputes between the United States and Britain over the Oregon Country
(3) relations with the Native American Indians of the Great Plains
(4) the role of the federal government in industrial development 11 ___

12. One reason the decision in *Dred Scott* v. *Sanford* (1857) was so controversial is that it
(1) strengthened the idea of popular sovereignty
(2) gave enslaved persons full citizenship
(3) ruled that Congress had no power to limit slavery in the territories
(4) supported Harriet Beecher Stowe's point of view in *Uncle Tom's Cabin* 12 ___

13. When Andrew Carnegie stated, "The man who dies rich, dies disgraced," he was supporting
(1) consumer credit   (3) Social Darwinism
(2) charitable giving   (4) antitrust legislation 13 ___

Base your answer to question 14 on the chart and on your knowledge of social studies.

Buffalo Population: 1800 to 1895

Date	Population
1800	40,000,000
1850	20,000,000
1865	15,000,000
1870	14,000,000
1875	1,000,000
1880	395,000
1885	20,000
1889	1,091
1895	Less than 1,000

Source: U.S. Department of Interior (adapted)

14. A major impact of the trend shown on the chart was that
(1) frontier trading posts became more prosperous
(2) Plains Indians lost their main source of food, shelter, and clothing
(3) reservations were relocated closer to buffalo migration routes
(4) white settlers became dependent on buffalo products

15. "A government's primary role is to provide a favorable atmosphere for business, including a stable currency, hands-off regulation, and domestic order." A supporter of this idea would most likely favor
(1) establishing consumer protection laws
(2) securing collective-bargaining rights
(3) levying high taxes on business
(4) following laissez-faire economics

Base your answer to question 16 on the photograph below and on your knowledge of social studies.

Source: Solomon Butcher, 1886

16. Which act of Congress most directly contributed to the situation shown in this photo?
(1) the Homestead Act
(2) the Sherman Antitrust Act
(3) the purchase of Alaska
(4) the Interstate Commerce Act

Base your answer to question 17 on the passage below and on your knowledge of social studies.

...We think the enforced separation of the races, as applied to the internal commerce of the State, neither abridges the privileges or immunities of the colored man, deprives him of his property without due process of law, nor denies him the equal protection of the laws within the meaning of the Fourteenth Amendment...

17. Which Supreme Court decision is reflected in this passage?
(1) *Wabash, St. Louis & Pacific R. R. v. Illinois* (1886)
(2) *United States v. E. C. Knight Co.* (1895)
(3) *In Re Debs* (1895)
(4) *Plessy v. Ferguson* (1896)

18. In the late 1800s, one reason labor unions struggled to gain support was because
(1) employers could easily replace striking employees
(2) the wages of industrial laborers were high
(3) government-funded public-works jobs were readily available
(4) corporations ended the use of court injunctions

19. Which term is most closely associated with the start of the Spanish-American War?
(1) socialism (2) populism (3) yellow journalism (4) isolationism

Base your answer to question 20 on the cartoon below and on your knowledge of social studies.

The Appearance of the New Party in the Political Field

Source: W. A. Carson, *Utica Saturday Globe*, 1912 (adapted)

20. What is the main idea of this 1912 cartoon?
(1) The Democratic Party is losing support.
(2) Republicans outnumber Democrats in the United States.
(3) The political process has no room for more than two parties.
(4) A third political party can threaten the two major parties.

21. In the late 1800s, the major goal of United States policy in both the annexation of Hawaii and the acquisition of the Philippines was to
(1) obtain coaling stations and seaports for United States ships
(2) expand United States fishing rights in international waters
(3) limit the spread of Japanese influence
(4) protect the area around the Panama Canal   21 ___

22. "**Income Tax Amendment Passes**"
    "**Congress Enacts Federal Reserve Act**"
    "**Pure Food and Drug Act Passed by Congress**"

    Which reform movement supported the actions described by these headlines?
    (1) Progressive   (2) Prohibition   (3) labor   (4) conservation   22 ___

23. In his war message to Congress, President Woodrow Wilson urged the United States to enter World War I in order to
(1) protect the empires of European countries
(2) create a new world government
(3) make the world safe for democracy
(4) stop a British attack on the United States   23 ___

Base your answer to question 24 on the cartoon and on your knowledge of social studies.

Step by Step

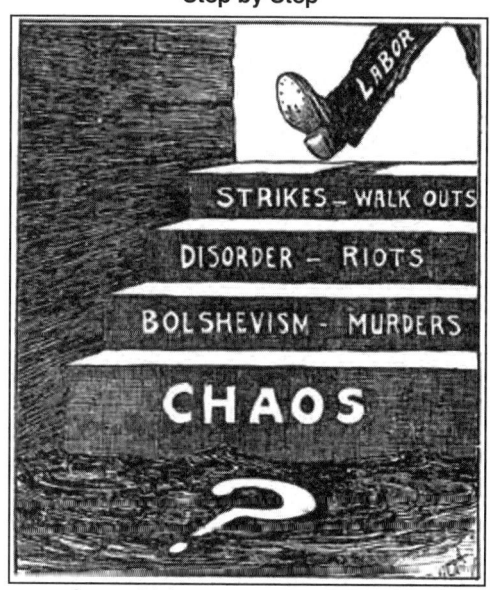

Source: Sid Greene, *New York Evening Telegram*, 1919 (adapted)

24. What is the cartoonist's point of view in this 1919 cartoon?
(1) Immigrants will easily assimilate into American society.
(2) Industrial production will expand and create more jobs.
(3) Civil liberties will be restricted and ordinary American citizens will be hurt.
(4) The actions of labor unions threaten the American way of life.   24 ___

Base your answer to question 25 on the photograph and on your knowledge of social studies.

25. This photograph shows one side of the 1920s conflict between

(1) union men and factory owners
(2) science and religion
(3) nativists and immigrants
(4) censorship and free press

Source: Photo taken in Dayton, Tennessee, 1925; University of Missouri-Kansas City, School of Law (adapted)

Base your answer to question 26 on the poem below and on your knowledge of social studies.

I, TOO

I, too, sing America.

I am the darker brother.
They send me to eat in the kitchen
When company comes,
But I laugh,
And eat well,
And grow strong.

Tomorrow,
I'll be at the table
When company comes.
Nobody'll dare
Say to me,
"Eat in the kitchen,"
Then.

Besides,
They'll see how beautiful I am
And be ashamed—

I, too, am America.

—Langston Hughes, "I, Too," 1926

26. During the 1920s, which development was most closely associated with this poem?
(1) growth of the motion-picture industry
(2) emergence of an antiwar party
(3) blossoming of African American culture
(4) expansion of mass consumption

27. In the 1920s, authors such as F. Scott Fitzgerald, Ernest Hemingway, and Sinclair Lewis wrote primarily about
(1) the intolerance of the Ku Klux Klan
(2) post–World War I disillusionment and materialism
(3) the failure of cultural pluralism
(4) the lack of educational opportunities for younger Americans   27 ___

28. The Federal Deposit Insurance Corporation (FDIC) and the Securities and Exchange Commission (SEC) were part of President Franklin D. Roosevelt's efforts to
(1) reduce the power of business monopolies during the Great Depression
(2) give organized labor a stronger voice in politics
(3) reform economic problems that contributed to the Great Depression
(4) bring electricity to rural areas   28 ___

29. President Franklin D. Roosevelt proposed a plan in 1937 to add justices to the Supreme Court primarily because the Court
(1) lacked representation from minority groups
(2) had declared major New Deal laws unconstitutional
(3) had little judicial experience
(4) supported a loose interpretation of the Constitution   29 ___

Base your answers to questions 30 and 31 on the graph and on your knowledge of social studies.

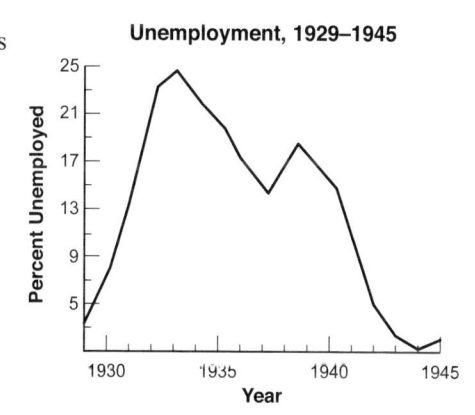

Unemployment, 1929–1945

Source: *Historical Statistics of the United States: Colonial Times to 1970*, U.S. Census Bureau, 1975 (adapted)

30. What was the major reason for the change in unemployment shown on the graph between 1933 and 1937?
(1) Banks increased their lending to new businesses, who hired more workers.
(2) The profits of corporations were heavily taxed by the states.
(3) Job opportunities were created by New Deal public-works projects.
(4) The federal government nationalized the transportation and utility industries.   30 ___

31. What was the main cause of the trend in employment shown on the graph between 1942 and 1945?
(1) increased manufacturing to meet the needs of World War II
(2) the success of the Social Security Act
(3) the impact of a high inflation rate
(4) a decline in the number of women in the work force   31 ___

32. The Neutrality Acts (1935–1937) were passed to
(1) support the policy of appeasement
(2) provide troops to halt Italian aggression
(3) increase the profits of United States weapons manufacturers
(4) avoid the actions that led the United States into World War I   32 ___

33. Which government action was a response to the Japanese attack on Pearl Harbor?
(1) drafting all Japanese American men into the United States Army
(2) passing labor laws banning the employment of immigrants
(3) ending all oil sales to Japan
(4) forcing the relocation and internment of Japanese Americans   33 ___

Base your answer to question 34 on the posters below and on your knowledge of social studies.

Source: New York State Works Progress Administration Art Project

Source: Office for Emergency Management

34. Which United States government action was most similar to the goal shown in these World War II posters?
(1) institution of the draft by the Selective Service Act (1940)
(2) aid to Russia under the Lend-Lease Act (1941)
(3) rationing by the Office of Price Administration (1941)
(4) development of the Manhattan Project (1942)   34 ___

35. The Servicemen's Readjustment Act of 1944 (GI Bill) made a significant impact on post–World War II America because it provided for
(1) aid to veterans for housing and college costs
(2) the rapid demobilization of soldiers
(3) pensions for soldiers from World War I
(4) the establishment of a draft for all males over 18 years of age   35 ___

36. Following World War II, the United States adopted the foreign policy of containment primarily to
(1) return to pre-war isolationism
(2) limit the spread of communism
(3) force European nations to end colonialism
(4) support the work of the World Court   36 ___

37. One important effect of President Eisenhower's proposal for interstate highways was a significant increase in
(1) health-care spending   (3) educational opportunities
(2) suburban communities   (4) sectional differences   37 ___

Base your answer to question 38 on the passage below and on your knowledge of social studies.

The people of the United States share with the people of the Soviet Union their satisfaction for the safe flight of the astronaut in man's first venture into space. We congratulate you and the Soviet scientists and engineers who made this feat possible. It is my sincere desire that in the continuing quest for knowledge of outer space our nations can work together to obtain the greatest benefit to mankind.
—President John F. Kennedy,
Telegram to Nikita Khrushchev, April 12, 1961

38. One way President Kennedy responded to the Soviet action referred to in the telegram was to support
(1) a decrease in the budget for space exploration
(2) an expansion of the Peace Corps to aid impoverished nations
(3) the removal of Soviet troops from East Berlin
(4) the commitment to a Moon landing by the end of the decade   38 ___

39. • Establishing a direct telephone line between Washington and Moscow
    • Negotiating a limited nuclear test-ban treaty
    • Selling surplus wheat to the Soviet Union

These actions by presidents John F. Kennedy and Richard Nixon are examples of their attempts to
(1) meet the Soviet Union's Cold War demands
(2) establish peaceful coexistence with the Soviet Union
(3) support Soviet troops fighting in Afghanistan
(4) weaken the military power of the Soviet Union   39 ___

40. During the 1960s, the escalation of United States involvement in the Vietnam War was based on the belief that
(1) restoring French colonial power was necessary for political stability in Southeast Asia
(2) a strong military presence would limit Japanese trade with Vietnam
(3) a North Vietnamese victory would lead to further losses as predicted by the domino theory
(4) a cease-fire agreement would increase college protests   40 ___

41. What was the major effect of the Civil Rights Act of 1964?
(1) Racial discrimination in public facilities was banned.
(2) Citizenship and voting rights were extended to Native American Indians.
(3) The use of poll taxes and literacy tests for voting were outlawed.
(4) Busing to integrate schools was authorized. 41 ___

42. Which pair of Supreme Court cases upheld the right to counsel for defendants in state criminal cases?
(1) *Mapp* v. *Ohio* (1961) and *Heart of Atlanta Motel* v. *United States* (1964)
(2) *Baker* v. *Carr* (1962) and *Engel* v. *Vitale* (1962)
(3) *Gideon* v. *Wainwright* (1963) and *Miranda* v. *Arizona* (1966)
(4) *Tinker* v. *Des Moines* (1969) and *Roe* v. *Wade* (1973) 42 ___

Base your answer to question 43 on the graph below and on your knowledge of social studies.

Percent of Men and Women in Labor Force: 1950 to 1990

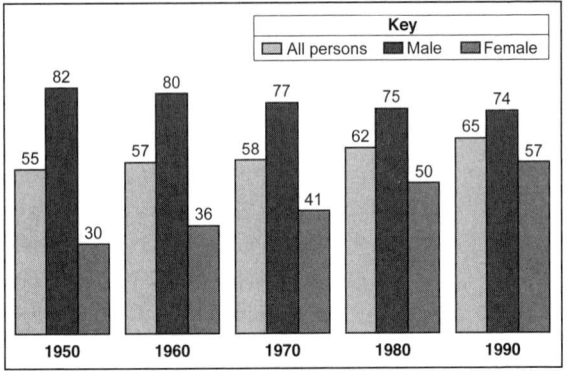

Key: All persons, Male, Female

Year	All persons	Male	Female
1950	55	82	30
1960	57	80	36
1970	58	77	41
1980	62	75	50
1990	65	74	57

Source: U.S. Census Bureau, 1990 (adapted)

43. Which conclusion is most clearly supported by information in the graph?
(1) Older Americans remained in the labor force longer in 1990 than in 1950.
(2) All Americans born during the baby boom after World War II joined the labor force.
(3) Half as many men were in the labor force in 1990 as compared to 1950.
(4) In every decade shown, the percentage of women in the labor force grew while the percentage of men in the labor force declined. 43 ___

44. During the Persian Gulf War (1991), the primary aim of the United States was to force Iraq to
(1) withdraw its troops from Kuwait
(2) hold democratic elections
(3) increase the price of its oil exports
(4) submit to weapons inspections by the United Nations 44 ___

45. In 1993, many labor union leaders opposed United States membership in the North American Free Trade Agreement (NAFTA) because they feared it would
(1) cause Americans to lose jobs to foreign nations
(2) reduce the number of immigrants to the United States
(3) result in higher exports from the United States to Mexico and Canada
(4) outlaw wage increases for workers in the United States 45 ___

Base your answer to question 46 on the cartoon and on your knowledge of social studies.

THE 9-11 HEARINGS...
BLAME

Source: Steve Breen, *San Diego Union-Tribune*, 2004 (adapted)

46. According to the cartoonist, the investigation of intelligence failures related to the 9/11 terrorist attacks resulted in
(1) praise for government efforts to stop intelligence leaks
(2) open immigration from all regions of the world
(3) recommendations to limit dependence on foreign intelligence
(4) various federal agencies attempting to avoid criticism by shifting responsibility   46 ___

47. Between 1881 and 1921, one major cause of the increasing number of immigrants to the United States was the
(1) availability of free land in the Southeast
(2) increased job opportunities in industry
(3) increased need for military personnel
(4) federal aid to pay the housing costs of new arrivals   47 ___

48. Prior to its military involvement in both the War of 1812 and World War I, the United States attempted to maintain a policy of
(1) neutrality
(2) internationalism
(3) collective security
(4) détente   48 ___

49. "...We conclude that, in the field of public education, the doctrine of 'separate but equal' has no place. Separate educational facilities are inherently unequal."...

These statements were included in which Supreme Court decision?
(1) *Schenck* v. *United States* (1919)
(2) *Korematsu* v. *United States* (1944)
(3) *Brown* v. *Board of Education of Topeka* (1954)
(4) *Vernonia School District* v. *Acton* (1995)   49 ___

50. • Alien and Sedition Acts of 1798
• Espionage Act of 1917
• USA Patriot Act of 2001

One common effect of these wartime laws has been to
(1) expand government regulation of the economy
(2) increase the nation's military defenses
(3) promote immigration from neighboring nations
(4) protect national security at the expense of civil liberties   50 ___

Part II
THEMATIC ESSAY QUESTION

Directions: Write a well-organized essay that includes an introduction, several paragraphs addressing the task below, and a conclusion.

Theme: Amendments

> The writers of the United States Constitution included an amending process to respond to changing times and unforeseen circumstances. Since the Civil War, important amendments have had an impact on the United States and/or on American society.

Task:

> Select *two* amendments to the United States Constitution *since* the Civil War and for *each*
> - Describe the historical circumstances surrounding the adoption of the amendment
> - Discuss the impact of this amendment on the United States and/or on American society

You may use any constitutional amendment that has been added *since* the Civil War. Some suggestions you might wish to consider include:

    13th amendment—abolition of slavery (1865)
    15th amendment—African American male suffrage (1870)
    16th amendment—graduated income tax (1913)
    17th amendment—direct election of United States senators (1913)
    18th amendment—Prohibition (1919)
    19th amendment—woman's suffrage (1920)
    26th amendment—18-year-old vote (1971)

You are *not* limited to these suggestions.

Guidelines:
In your essay, be sure to:
- Develop all aspects of the task
- Support the theme with relevant facts, examples, and details
- Use a logical and clear plan of organization, including an introduction and a conclusion that are beyond a restatement of the theme

Part III
DOCUMENT-BASED QUESTION

This question is based on the accompanying documents. The question is designed to test your ability to work with historical documents. Some of these documents have been edited for the purposes of this question. As you analyze the documents, take into account the source of each document and any point of view that may be presented in the document. Keep in mind that the language and images used in a document may reflect the historical context of the time in which it was created.

U. S. HISTORY — August 2019

Historical Context:
The president of the United States has been granted power as the commander in chief by the Constitution. Although the president has used his military powers to commit troops overseas, he has also used this power to respond to domestic challenges. These challenges have included ***President Grover Cleveland and the Pullman strike, President Herbert Hoover and the Bonus Army,*** and ***President Harry Truman and segregation in the armed forces***

Task: Using information from the documents and your knowledge of United States history, answer the questions that follow each document in Part A. Your answers to the questions will help you write the Part B essay in which you will be asked to

> Choose *two* domestic challenges mentioned in the historical context and for *each*
> • Describe the historical circumstances that led to the president's action
> • Discuss how the president's action influenced the United States and/or American society

Part A
Short-Answer Questions

Directions: **Analyze the documents and answer the short-answer questions that follow each document in the space provided.**

Document 1

> The Pullman Strike of 1894 was the first national strike in United States history. Before coming to an end, it involved over 150,000 persons and twenty-seven states and territories and would paralyze the nation's railway system. The entire rail labor force of the nation would walk away from their jobs. In supporting the capital side [railroad owners] of this strike President Cleveland for the first time in the Nation's history would send in federal troops, who would fire on and kill United States Citizens, against the wishes of the states. The federal courts of the nation would outlaw striking by the passing of the Omnibus indictment [federal charges against the leaders of the American Railway Union]. This blow to unionized labor would not be struck down until the passing of the Wagner act in 1935. This all began in the little town of Pullman, Illinois, just south of Chicago. . . .
>
> Source: Keith Ladd and Greg Rickman, "The Pullman Strike," kansasheritage.org, 1998 (adapted)

1. According to Keith Ladd and Greg Rickman, what was *one* effect of President Cleveland's decision to support railroad owners during the Pullman strike? [1]

_____

_____

Document 2

The nation's worst depression of the 19th century began in 1893. In 1894, the worst year of the depression, workers at the Pullman Company went on strike in Chicago.

> ... The rents Pullman charged were excessive, running about 25 percent higher than in neighboring towns. He sold at ten cents per thousand gallons water that he bought from Chicago at four cents. He forced his tenants to buy their food and other necessities from company stores, where prices far exceeded those of regular outlets. The simmering cauldron of protest boiled over when in 1894 the company cut wages an average of 25 percent, without a comparable cut in rent or in the cost of necessities. Pullman refused to listen to complaints and dismissed from their jobs those who persisted in the outcry. He then closed the plant.
>
> At this juncture [time], the American Railway Union, which had a membership of 150,000, including several thousand Pullman employees, joined the struggle, ordering its members not to handle trains with Pullman cars attached. The strike was quickly turned into a national disruption. Within a month, railroad traffic, particularly in the western states, was almost at a standstill. The beset [besieged] railroad owners hit on the scheme of coupling Pullman cars to trains that carried mail, confident that any interference with the mail was a federal crime. When the strikers still refused to man the trains, the railroads persuaded Attorney General Olney to swear in an army of special deputies—actually in the pay of the railroads—in order to help keep the trains moving.
>
> The leader of the union was Eugene V. Debs, a gentle but dynamic person who had made the interests of workingmen the consuming enthusiasm of his life. He had instructed his members to avoid violence. But it broke out now anyhow between the deputies and the strikers. The railroads in their frustration asked President Cleveland to send federal troops to keep order and to guarantee the safe handling of the mails. ...

Source: Henry F. Graff, *Grover Cleveland*, Henry Holt and Company, 2002

2*a*. According to Henry F. Graff, what was *one* reason Pullman workers went on strike? [1]

_____
_____
_____

2*b*. According to Henry F. Graff, what was *one* reason President Grover Cleveland was asked to send federal troops to Chicago? [1]

_____
_____
_____

Document 3a

President Grover Cleveland responded to the strike and to the riots that followed by sending federal troops to Chicago.

> . . . Cleveland also feared the worst, and responded accordingly. Federal troops arrived to quell [stop] the riots, ironically, on July 4. While patriotic citizens set off fireworks, in the city of Chicago they set fires. Thousands of angry protestors lay waste to the city. At the Chicago rail yards more freight trains were flipped over and cars set ablaze. A huge fire that night destroyed the expositions on the grounds of the World's Fair. Chicago degenerated into lawlessness and chaos.
>
> It continued for four days. On July 6, a rail deputy shot two men, inciting the largest riot of all—6,000 rail workers destroyed over $340,000 worth of railroad property on a single day as over 700 railroad cars were torched. The next day, a mob attacked the state militia. The soldiers fired back, killing 4 rioters and wounding 20 others. Reinforcements for the federal troops were called up from surrounding states. No American city had ever experienced such anarchy in peacetime. . . .

Source: Source: Chris Wallace, *Character: Profiles in Presidential Courage*, Rugged Land, 2004

Document 3b

Burning of Six Hundred Freight-Cars on the Panhandle Railroad, South of Fiftieth Street, on the Evening of July 6th.

Source: Source: G. A. Coffin and Charles Mente, *Harper's Weekly*, July 21, 1894

3. Based on these documents, what was *one* effect of President Cleveland's decision to send federal troops to end the Pullman strike? [1]

_____

_____

Document 4a Veterans' sheds, tents, and shanties sprawled across the Anacostia Flats in Washington, D.C., in 1932.

Source: National Archives (adapted)

Document 4b
Violent clash between police and veterans on the morning of July 28, 1932.

Source: General Douglas MacArthur Foundation

Document 4c

...No "civil commotion" attracted as much attention as the march of the "bonus army." Demanding immediate and full payment of bonuses for their service in World War I, 15,000 to 20,000 unemployed veterans moved on Washington in the spring of 1932. The House passed the bonus bill, but when the Senate voted it down by an overwhelming margin, half the men stayed on; they had no jobs, no homes, no place else to go. Most of them lived in mean shanties on the muddy Anacostia flats, some camped in unused government buildings. General Glassford, the head of the District police, treated the men decently and with discretion, but, as the men stayed on day after day, federal officials panicked. On July 28, 1932, the government decided precipitately [suddenly] to evict bonus marchers from vacant buildings on Pennsylvania Avenue. Two veterans were killed and several District police were injured in a scuffle that followed. President Hoover summoned the U.S. Army to take over....

Source: William E. Leuchtenburg, *The Perils of Prosperity, 1914–1932*, University of Chicago Press, 1993

4*a*. Based on these documents, state *one* reason World War I veterans marched on Washington, D.C., in 1932. [1]

_____

_____

4*b*. Based on these documents, state *one* reason President Hoover sent the United States Army to remove the Bonus Marchers. [1]

_____

_____

Document 5a

The Washington Post
WASHINGTON: FRIDAY, JULY 29, 1932.

ONE SLAIN, 60 HURT AS TROOPS ROUT B. E. F. WITH GAS BOMBS AND FLAMES

Troops Burn Bonus Billets in Shadow of Capital as Rout Begins

ANACOSTIA HUTS FIRED; MEN ARE DENIED RIGHT TO RETURN TO CAPITAL

All Bonus Groups in Western Section of Capital Are Evicted Amid Disorder.

CONCERTED DRIVE FOLLOWS HOOVER EDICT FOR ACTION

Shacks in Pennsylvania Avenue Area Are Also Burned; Reserve Police Added at White House.

By DANIEL R. MAHER.

Tear gas bombs and torches, unleashed by Federal troops in a sweeping offensive, routed the ragged bonus army yesterday from every major encampment in the Capital in a day of wild disorder that took the life of one veteran.

In a relentless drive, infantrymen, cavalrymen and tanks opened the drive against the veterans on Pennsylvania avenue, herded them from the Southwest section and stopped their offensive at Camp Marks, the largest of the bonus army encampments.

In front of Camp Marks, Chief of Staff Douglas A. MacArthur, on orders from a high authority, ordered pontoons of the drive, but it was needless, for the 5,000 veterans in the camp were in full retreat. They set fire to their rude shacks and early today the flames were burning a memorial across the sky in what may be the epitaph of the bonus army.

More Than 60 Hurt in Clashes.

Though peace again reigned, the hospitals held the more than 60 suffering victims of the series of clashes that forced...

Source: Washington Post, Friday, July 29, 1932

Document 5b

... A storm of protest followed. Americans who viewed the photographs and read the reports over the next few days found the actions of their government inexcusable. Any remaining faith they still had in Washington was now called into question, especially when Hoover and MacArthur attempted to justify their orders by saying that the marchers were criminals and communists. Far from a revolutionary crowd, the veterans seemed to most people to be little different than the rest of the nation: they had no work and they wanted to feed their families. Squeezed from all directions, the people needed an ally—desperately —and in the Democratic candidate for president in 1932, they finally found one. . . .

Source: Peter Jennings and Todd Brewster, *The Century*, Doubleday, 1998

5. According to these documents, what were *two* reasons many Americans thought the government's action against the veterans was wrong? [2]

(1) _____

(2) _____

Document 6

...American history is punctuated by moments and incidents that become prisms through which larger events are better understood—the Boston Tea Party, Nat Turner's Rebellion, the Alamo, John Brown's Raid. The march of the Bonus Army belongs in such company. But its significance has been obscured [dimmed] by time, even to its direct beneficiaries—the millions of later veterans whose bonus would be the GI Bill and the benefits that have followed to the present day. And, its legacy is everlasting. The First Amendment of the Constitution grants Americans the right "to petition the government for redress of grievances." Millions of Americans have since peacefully marched on Washington in support of various causes, their way paved by the veterans of 1932.

Source: Paul Dickson and Thomas B. Allen, *The Bonus Army: An American Epic*, Walker and Company, 2004

6. According to Paul Dickson and Thomas B. Allen, what was *one* impact of the Bonus Army? [1]

Document 7

...The military's last all-black unit disbanded in 1954, and the services, with the exception of the navy, which lagged somewhat behind, recruited African Americans for all specialties. Acceptance in the ranks did not, however, mean acceptance in communities adjacent to military installations. While black service personnel had equal access to integrated military family quarters on bases, they faced the same discrimination in housing in local civilian communities that had always existed....

Black military personnel also faced discrimination in furthering their own education. Universities near military installations, especially in the South, refused to accept black students.

Outside the gates of their bases, black military personnel found that civilian communities treated them in the same manner as they did their local minority population. Jim Crow laws, again mostly in the South but to some degree throughout the country, separated black from white in shopping, eating, housing, transportation, and recreational facilities. Frequently these public areas exhibited Whites Only signs, and the towns had police more than willing to enforce these policies....

The arrival of the 1960s brought increased impatience in the black military and civilian communities. Protests continued, with sit-ins the dominant form of nonviolent action as blacks and their supporters challenged local Jim Crow laws restricting their access to eating establishments and other public facilities....

Source: Lt. Colonel (Ret.) Michael Lee Lanning, *The African-American Soldier: From Crispus Attucks to Colin Powell*, Citadel Press, 2004 (adapted)

7. According to Michael Lee Lanning, what was *one* way discrimination against African Americans continued after President Truman's executive order? [1]

Document 8a

In 1941, civil rights activist A. Philip Randolph demanded an end to racial segregation in the Armed Forces.

... Roosevelt ignored Randolph's call for a desegregated army. By that time, all branches of the military separated black soldiers into their own units, deployed them on segregated trains, and housed them in old, dilapidated barracks. Most black soldiers served as stewards and cooks or performed menial labor such as maintaining latrines [bathrooms]. As late as 1940, the U.S. armed services included only five black commissioned officers, including Benjamin O. Davis, Sr., the first African-American to reach the rank of general, and Benjamin O. Davis, Jr., the 20th century's first black graduate of West Point. Military leaders routinely denied black soldiers entry into many training classes that would have enabled them to advance in rank. ...

Source: Mark Bauerlein et al., *Civil Rights Chronicle: The African American Struggle for Freedom*, Legacy, 2003

Document 8b

... Not surprisingly, black organizations pressed hard for equality within the armed services. They viewed the military as a key institution in American life. A direct arm of the government, and a direct expression of the people, it personified the democratic values for which the United States fought. Ending racial discrimination in the armed forces would have a powerful effect on civil society. Moreover, if blacks made an equal contribution to the war effort, their claim to full citizenship would be much stronger. ...

Source: Adam Fairclough, *Better Day Coming: Blacks and Equality, 1890–2000*, Viking, 2001,

8. Based on these documents, what were *two* reasons African American civil rights leaders called for an end to racial segregation in the Armed Forces? [2]

(1)_____

_____

_____

(2)_____

_____

_____

Document 9a

Following World War II, on orders from President Truman, the Army, Navy, and Air Force abolished their traditional Jim Crow units and with very little fanfare integrated themselves. On a recent [September 1963] 3,200-mile tour of the South, we viewed the impressive results.

We saw Negro and white servicemen eating at the same mess-hall tables, drinking at the same on-base bars, playing ball on the same teams. They sleep in the same barracks, share lavatories and showers, borrow money from one another until pay day.

In on-base homes assigned without regard for race, white and Negro families live next door to one another, baby-sit for one another, watch TV together, share backyard barbecues. They swim together in on-base pools, worship together in military chapels. Their children play and squabble happily together on the lawns, attend on-base schools and Sunday schools together. All this has for years been accepted practice on military bases, including many in the Deep South. . . .

Source: Ruth and Edward Brecher, "The Military's Limited War Against Segregation," *Reporting Civil Rights,* The Library of America

Document 9b
Soldiers from the U.S. Army's Integrated Second Infantry Division in Korea

Source: Defense Media Network (adapted)

9. Based on these documents, what were *two* results of President Harry Truman's executive order abolishing segregated "Jim Crow units" in the military? [2]

(1) _____

(2) _____

U. S. HISTORY — August 2019

Part B
Essay

Directions: Write a well-organized essay that includes an introduction, several paragraphs, and a conclusion. Use evidence from *at least four* documents in the body of the essay. Support your response with relevant facts, examples, and details. Include additional outside information.

Historical Context:

The president of the United States has been granted power as the commander in chief by the Constitution. Although the president has used his military powers to commit troops overseas, he has also used this power to respond to domestic challenges. These challenges have included **President Grover Cleveland and the Pullman strike, President Herbert Hoover and the Bonus Army,** and **President Harry Truman and segregation in the armed forces.**

Task: Using information from the documents and your knowledge of United States history, write an essay in which you

> Choose *two* domestic challenges mentioned in the historical context and for *each*
> - Describe the historical circumstances that led to the president's action
> - Discuss how the president's action influenced the United States and/or American society

Guidelines:

In your essay, be sure to
- Develop all aspects of the task
- Incorporate information from *at least four* documents
- Incorporate relevant outside information
- Support the theme with relevant facts, examples, and details
- Use a logical and clear plan of organization, including an introduction and a conclusion that are beyond a restatement of the theme

U. S. HISTORY
January 2020
Part I

Answer all questions in this part.

Directions (1–50): For each statement or question, write on the space provided the *number* of the word or expression that, of those given, best completes the statement or answers the question.

Base your answer to question 1 on the map below and on your knowledge of social studies.

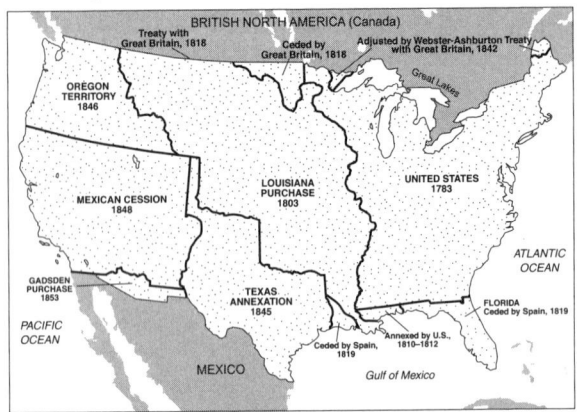

Source: Robert A. Divine, et al., *America: Past and Present*, Addison Wesley Longman, 1999 (adapted)

1. Most of the northern boundary of the United States was created by treaties between the United States and
(1) France (2) Great Britain (3) Spain (4) Mexico 1 _____

2. In colonial America, geography most directly influenced
(1) religious practices (3) economic activities
(2) voter eligibility (4) family structure 2 _____

3. European Enlightenment writers of the 17th and 18th centuries such as John Locke influenced America's colonial development by providing
(1) justification for state-supported churches
(2) a defense of the slave trade
(3) arguments for monarchy and rule by divine right
(4) ideas about self-government and political rights 3 _____

4. Which document encouraged public support for declaring independence from Great Britain?
(1) Albany Plan of Union (3) Alien and Sedition Acts
(2) Virginia and Kentucky Resolutions (4) *Common Sense* 4 _____

5. What was a major success of the national government under the Articles of Confederation (1781-1788)?
(1) developing a plan for the admission of new states
(2) establishing the first national export tax
(3) paying off all government debts
(4) gaining the respect of foreign nations 5 _____

6. Which statement best illustrates the meaning of federalism?
(1) All citizens enjoy the basic rights of freedom of speech, press, religion, and assembly.
(2) The Constitution delegates certain powers to the national government but reserves other powers for the states.
(3) The Constitution can be changed by amendments ratified by Congress.
(4) The House of Representatives has the power to impeach the president, and the Senate has the power to conduct an impeachment trial.   6 _____

7. The authors of the United States Constitution established a bicameral legislature primarily because they
(1) wished states to retain their absolute sovereignty
(2) reached a compromise between the large states and the small states over representation
(3) hoped to weaken the power of Congress
(4) wanted to create an independent judiciary elected by the people   7 _____

Base your answers to questions 8 and 9 on the passage below and on your knowledge of social studies.

... But the great security against a gradual concentration of the several powers in the same department, consists in giving to those who administer each department, the necessary constitutional means, and personal motives, to resist encroachments of the others. The provision for defence must in this, as in all other cases, be made commensurate [corresponding] to the danger of attack Ambition must be made to counteract ambition....
— James Madison, *The Federalist No. 51*, 1788

8. In this passage, James Madison argues for the governing principle known as
(1) checks and balances   (3) executive privilege
(2) representative government   (4) popular sovereignty   8 _____

9. Madison was one of the statesmen who wrote articles for *The Federalist* primarily to
(1) encourage rebellion against the British
(2) find a permanent solution to the issue of slavery
(3) gain support for ratifying the United States Constitution
(4) oppose protection of property rights in the United States Constitution   9 _____

Base your answer to question 10 on the passage below and on your knowledge of social studies.

... The great rule of conduct for us in regard to foreign nations is, in extending our commercial relations, to have with them as little *political* connection as possible. So far as we have already formed engagements, let them be fulfilled with perfect good faith. Here let us stop...,
— George Washington, Farewell Address, 1796

10. President George Washington made this statement in response to concerns over United States involvement in the
(1) effort to end the slave trade in West Africa
(2) struggle to open Asian ports to foreign trade
(3) independence movements of the new Latin American nations
(4) continuing conflict between England and France   10 _____

11. The establishment of judicial review in *Marbury v. Madison* (1803) gave the Supreme Court the authority to
(1) impeach members of Congress
(2) create state courts
(3) approve foreign treaties
(4) decide the constitutionality of a law   11 ___

12. The Supreme Court decisions in *McCulloch v. Maryland* (1819) and *Gibbons v. Ogden* (1824) were important because they
(1) increased the power of the federal government
(2) expanded the powers of the president
(3) encouraged westward expansion
(4) placed limits on the spread of slavery   12 ___

13. In the 1840s and 1850s, immigration to the United States was characterized by
(1) large numbers of immigrants from Latin America
(2) significant job opportunities for immigrants in southern states
(3) a large influx of Irish and German immigrants
(4) widespread acceptance of immigrants by native-born Americans   13 ___

Base your answer to question 14 on the passage below and on your knowledge of social studies.

... As to the policy I "seem to be pursuing" as you say, I have not meant to leave any one in doubt.

I would save the Union. I would save it the shortest way under the Constitution. The sooner the national authority can be restored; the nearer the Union will be "the Union as it was." If there be those who would not save the Union, unless they could at the same time *save* slavery, I do not agree with them. If there be those who would not save the Union unless they could at the same time *destroy* slavery, I do not agree with them. My paramount object in this struggle is to save the Union, and is *not* either to save or to destroy slavery. If I could save the Union without freeing *any* slave I would do it, and if I could save it by freeing *all* the slaves I would do it; and if I could save it by freeing some and leaving others alone I would also do that. What I do about slavery, and the colored race, I do because I believe it helps to save the Union; and what I forbear, I forbear because I do *not* believe it would help to save the Union. I shall do *less* whenever I shall believe what I am doing hurts the cause, and I shall do *more* whenever I shall believe doing more will help the cause. I shall try to correct errors whenshown to be errors; and I shall adopt new views so fast as they shall appear to be true views....

— President Abraham Lincoln, Letter to Horace Greeley, August 22, 1862

14. According to the passage, President Abraham Lincoln's primary goal in fighting the Civil War was to
(1) advance the cause of Northern abolitionists
(2) use any means necessary to save the Union
(3) extend the franchise to African Americans in the army
(4) free only those African Americans who were enslaved in Confederate territory   14 ___

15. Which geographic factor most directly influenced the rapid settlement of the Great Plains after the Civil War?
(1) immense forests for lumber
(2) access to abundant quantities of oil
(3) huge amounts of fertile farmland
(4) long ocean coastline with deep ports

15 ___

16. What was one reason the 14th and 15th amendments failed to prevent future racial segregation?
(1) Most Northern abolitionists opposed the extension of these rights.
(2) The Supreme Court refused to accept cases to interpret these amendments.
(3) Radical Republicans in Congress stopped African Americans from voting.
(4) The South was allowed to pass Jim Crow laws and restrict voting rights.

16 ___

Base your answers to questions 17 and 18 on the speakers' statements below and on your knowledge of social studies.

Speaker A: The time of unlimited immigration is now past; controls are necessary to preserve the customs and values that have made this nation great.

Speaker B: In order to protect our citizens' jobs, restrictions must be placed on the number of immigrants.

Speaker C: More workers are needed. The most important consideration is whether they are willing to work hard.

Speaker D: There's plenty of land left to settle in the West, and there is plenty of room for all.

17. Which two speakers would most likely have supported the Chinese Exclusion Act (1882)?
(1) *A* and *B*   (2) *B* and *C*   (3) *C* and *D*   (4) *A* and *D*

17 ___

18. Which speaker would most likely agree with the economic point of view of big business owners in the late 1800s?
(1) *A*   (2) *B*   (3) *C*   (4) *D*

18 ___

19. In the late 19th century, what was the major goal in developing the "New South?"
(1) expanding the industrial base
(2) reducing tobacco production
(3) strengthening labor unions
(4) restricting government support for railroad construction

19 ___

20. "Senate Votes to Annex Philippines"
"U.S. Sends Warships to Panama"
"President Roosevelt Strengthens Monroe Doctrine"

These headlines reflect the transformation of United States foreign policy into one that
(1) respected the sovereign rights of all countries
(2) practiced imperialism
(3) pursued isolationist policies
(4) opposed free-trade agreements

20 ___

21. What was the major goal of the political reforms enacted during the Progressive Era (1900-1920)?
(1) expanding citizen participation in government
(2) lowering the legal voting age
(3) discouraging the formation of new political parties
(4) providing public funding of campaigns

Base your answer to question 22 on the photograph and on your knowledge of social studies.

Dens of Death

22. Whose work most influenced state and local governments to address the conditions shown in this photograph?
(1) John Muir
(2) Ida Tarbell
(3) Frank Norris
(4) Jacob Riis

Source: *The Battle with the Slum*, MacMillan, 1902 (adapted)

23. The Meat Inspection Act (1906), the Pure Food and Drug Act (1906), and the Clayton Antitrust Act (1914) were similar in that each
(1) increased government regulation of business
(2) resulted from a pro-business government policy
(3) lowered tariffs on imported goods
(4) decreased federal taxes on personal income

24. The Federal Reserve System, created in 1913, extended government control over the banking system by
(1) issuing housing and consumer loans
(2) regulating interest rates and the money supply
(3) ending private ownership of banks
(4) banning loans for stock market purchases

Base your answer to question 25 on the photograph below and on your knowledge of social studies.

25. Actions such as the one shown in the photograph helped lead to the
(1) defeat of Germany in World War I
(2) failure of President Woodrow Wilson to win reelection
(3) rejection of United States membership in the League of Nations
(4) addition of a woman's suffrage amendment to the United States Constitution

KAISER WILSON

HAVE YOU FORGOTTEN YOUR SYMPATHY WITH THE POOR GERMANS BECAUSE THEY WERE NOT SELF-GOVERNED?

20,000,000 AMERICAN WOMEN ARE NOT SELF-GOVERNED

TAKE THE BEAM OUT OF YOUR OWN EYE.

26. Which term from the 1920s is most closely associated with Duke Ellington and Langston Hughes?
(1) Lost Generation
(2) Red Scare
(3) Teapot Dome scandal
(4) Harlem Renaissance

26 ___

27. Federal economic policies during the 1920s contributed to the start of the Great Depression by
(1) failing to adequately regulate stock market transactions
(2) adopting federal budgets with large deficits
(3) lowering protective tariffs
(4) abolishing corporate income taxes

27 ___

Base your answer to question 28 on the passage below and on your knowledge of social studies.

... But in the event that the Congress shall fail to take one of these two courses, and in the event that the national emergency is still critical, I shall not evade the clear course of duty that will then confront me. I shall ask the Congress for the one 'remaining instrument to meet the crisis—broad Executive power to wage a war against the emergency, as great as the power that would be given to me if we were in fact invaded by a foreign foe....
— President Franklin D. Roosevelt, First Inaugural Address, March 4, 1933

28. President Franklin D. Roosevelt dealt with the emergency referred to in this speech primarily by
(1) submitting problems to the Supreme Court
(2) relying on state and local governments to handle the situation
(3) gaining congressional support for his programs
(4) requesting financial assistance from other countries

28 ___

29. The main goal of the first Agricultural Adjustment Act (AAA) was to
(1) end wasteful funding of irrigation projects
(2) increase efforts to export grain
(3) encourage more farm mechanization
(4) stabilize farm prices by reducing the amount of surplus crops

29 ___

Base your answer to question 30 on the poem below and on your knowledge of social studies.

...We'll be back when it rains,
they say,
setting out with their bedsprings and mattresses,
their cookstoves and dishes,
their kitchen tables,
and their milk goats
tied to their running boards
in rickety cages,
setting out for
California,
where even though they say they'll come back,
they might just stay
if what they hear about that place is true....
— Karen Hesse, *Out of the Dust*, April 1935

30. What was the main reason for the migration described in this poem?
(1) Farmers were given inexpensive, fertile land in the West.
(2) An extended drought on the plains forced farmers to seek better conditions in the West.
(3) Manufacturing jobs in California paid high wages.
(4) African Americans left the South to avoid discrimination.   30 ___

Base your answer to question 31 on the cartoon and on your knowledge of social studies.

Source: J. N. "Ding" Darling, *Bridgeport Telegram*, March 29, 1937 (adapted)

31. This cartoon suggests that Congress believed President Franklin D. Roosevelt's proposals concerning the Supreme Court threatened the United States Constitution by
(1) weakening the system of federalism
(2) ignoring the amendment process
(3) endangering the principle of separation of powers
(4) violating the elastic clause   31 ___

32. During the 1930s, the major foreign policy goal of the United States Congress was to
(1) avoid the mistakes that led the country into World War I
(2) end the Good Neighbor policy
(3) increase the size of the armed forces
(4) strengthen support for Japan's New Order in Asia   32 ___

33. The primary reason President Harry Truman made the decision to use atomic bombs on Hiroshima and Nagasaki was to
(1) save American lives by avoiding the invasion of Japan
(2) destroy the entire Japanese military in Southeast Asia
(3) allow the United States to defeat Germany
(4) halt the Japanese invasion of the Soviet Union   33 ___

34. Organizing the Berlin airlift, implementing the Marshall Plan, and fighting the Korean War were early events in the United States policy of
(1) imperialism   (2) containment   (3) isolationism   (4) neutrality   34 ___

35. In the late 1940s, hearings by the House Committee on Un-American Activities and the use of loyalty oaths illustrate concerns over the
(1) impact of union strikes on the economy
(2) United States participation in the North Atlantic Treaty Organization (NATO)
(3) desegregation of the military
(4) influence of communists within the federal government   35 ___

36. The Korean War (1950–1953) was the first war in which the United States
(1) sent troops to fight on foreign soil
(2) responded to an attack on its homeland
(3) fought as a member of United Nations forces
(4) formed an alliance with mainland China   36 ___

Base your answer to question 37 on the passage below and on your knowledge of social studies.

... Finally, you have broader considerations that might follow what you would call the "falling domino" principle. You have a row of dominoes set up, you knock over the first one, and what will happen to the last one is the certainty that it will go over very quickly. So you could have a beginning of a disintegration that would have the most profound influences....

— President Dwight D. Eisenhower, April 7, 1954

37. Which action is most closely associated with the foreign policy concern expressed by President Dwight D. Eisenhower in this passage?
(1) authorizing U-2 flights over the Soviet Union
(2) increasing United States involvement in Vietnam
(3) overthrowing military dictatorships in Central America
(4) defending oil producing countries in the Middle East   37 ___

38. The actions of Jackie Robinson, Rosa Parks, and Malcolm X helped focus national attention on the need for reform in the area of
(1) environmental protection   (3) public education
(2) crime prevention   (4) civil rights   38 ___

39. Which statement best describes an outcome of the 1962 Cuban missile crisis?
(1) Communist leaders of Cuba were removed from office.
(2) The United States strengthened its ties with Cuba.
(3) Nuclear war with the Soviet Union was avoided.
(4) United States military defenses were significantly reduced.   39 ___

40. *Mapp v. Ohio* (1961), *Gideon v Wainwright* (1963), and *Miranda v. Arizona* (1966) are all Supreme Court decisions that strengthened individual rights by
(1) increasing protections for persons accused of crimes
(2) eliminating restrictions on gun ownership
(3) overturning racial segregation laws
(4) encouraging greater voter participation in government   40 ___

41. President Richard Nixon chose to resign the presidency mainly because of his involvement in the
(1) secret bombing of Cambodia
(2) escalation of the Vietnam War
(3) Watergate scandal
(4) implementation of wage-price controls

41 ___

42. In *Tinker* v. *Des Moines School District* (1969) and in *New Jersey* v. *T.L.O.* (1985), the United States Supreme Court addressed the
(1) issue of gender equality in school athletics
(2) recitation of prayers in public schools
(3) power of school authorities to determine curriculum
(4) free speech and privacy rights of students in schools

42 ___

43. Results of the Bush-Gore presidential election of 2000 renewed the debate over
(1) term limits for elected officials
(2) the electoral college system
(3) presidential use of the veto power
(4) loose versus strict interpretation of the Constitution

43 ___

Base your answer to question 44 on the map below and on your knowledge of social studies.

Change in House of Representatives Based on 2010 Census

Source: U. S. Census Bureau (adapted)

44. The gains and losses shown on the map were primarily the result of
(1) population changes among the states
(2) migration of African Americans to the North
(3) vacancies in the House of Representatives caused by resignations
(4) increasing the total number of members in the House of Representatives

44 ___

Base your answer to question 45 on the chart and on your knowledge of social studies.

USA SNAPSHOTS©

'Oldest old' crowd growing rapidly

Americans 85 and over, in millions:

- 2011: 5.0
- 2020: 6.7
- 2030: 8.9
- 2050: 18.0

*2020–2050 are projections

Source: *USA Today*, February 4, 2013 (adapted)

45. Which government programs will be most directly affected by the trend shown on this chart?
(1) defense spending
(2) immigration reform
(3) Head Start and school construction
(4) Medicare and Social Security   45 ___

46. "Same-Sex Marriage Upheld by Supreme Court"
    "47% of Children Live With One Parent"
    "Majority of College Degrees Now Go to Women"

A conclusion that can be drawn directly from these headlines is that
(1) more people are delaying marriage to a later age
(2) legal and societal changes have affected the family unit
(3) the role of women has changed little in the past decade
(4) most married couples do not have children   46 ___

47. Which statement reflects a major transportation trend of the post–World War II period?
(1) Transcontinental railroads were developed.
(2) The use of canals to move freight increased.
(3) The use of the automobile increased dramatically.
(4) Air travel decreased significantly.   47 ___

48. One way in which the Truman Doctrine and the Eisenhower Doctrine are similar is that both
(1) offered aid to countries threatened by communism
(2) attempted to create a friendlier relationship with China
(3) tried to improve relations with the Soviet Union
(4) returned the United States to an isolationist foreign policy   48 ___

49. The programs of President Lyndon B. Johnson's War on Poverty had goals which were most similar to the programs of
(1) Theodore Roosevelt's Square Deal
(2) Woodrow Wilson's New Freedom
(3) Franklin D. Roosevelt's New Deal
(4) Ronald Reagan's New Federalism   49 ___

50. Which pair of economic situations faced both President Franklin D. Roosevelt and President Barack Obama during the first 100 days of their administrations?
(1) legalization of the sale of alcoholic beverages and suspension of antitrust laws
(2) high unemployment and failures in the banking system
(3) funding overseas wars and bailing out the automobile industry
(4) modifying the gold standard and increasing federal aid to education 50 ___

In developing your answer to Part II, keep these definitions in mind:
  (a) **explain** means "to make plain or understandable; to give reasons for or causes of; to show the logical development or relationships of"
  (b) **discuss** means "to make observations about something using facts, reasoning, and argument; to present in some detail"

Part II
THEMATIC ESSAY QUESTION

Directions: Write a well-organized essay that includes an introduction, several paragraphs addressing the task below, and a conclusion.

Theme: Foreign Policy

> Throughout United States history, the government has taken foreign policy actions that have resulted in differences of opinion among the American people. These actions have had impacts on the United States and on other countries and regions.

Task:

> Select *two* foreign policy actions that have caused disagreement among the American people and for *each*
> - Explain the point of view of those who *supported* the foreign policy action
> - Explain the point of view of those who *opposed* the foreign policy action
> - Discuss the impact of the action on the United States *and/or* on another country or region

You may use any foreign policy action that caused disagreement among the American people. Some suggestions you might wish to consider include purchasing Louisiana (1803), declaring war against Mexico (1846), purchasing Alaska (1867), annexing the Philippines (1899), maintaining neutrality in World War I (1914-1917), providing Lend-Lease aid to Great Britain (1941), sending troops to Vietnam (1964-1973), ratifying the North American Free Trade Agreement (1993), and implementing Operation Iraqi Freedom (2003).

You are *not* limited to these suggestions.

Guidelines:

In your essay, be sure to:
- Develop all aspects of the task
- Support the theme with relevant facts, examples, and details
- Use a logical and clear plan of organization, including an introduction and a conclusion that are beyond a restatement of the theme

U. S. HISTORY — January 2020   89

In developing your answers to Part III, keep these definitions in mind:
  (a) **describe** means "to illustrate something in words or tell about it"
  (b) **discuss** means "to make observations about something using facts, reasoning, and argument; to present in some detail"

Part III
DOCUMENT-BASED QUESTION

This question is based on the accompanying documents. The question is designed to test your ability to work with historical documents. Some of these documents have been edited for the purposes of this question. As you analyze the documents, take into account the source of each document and any point of view that may be presented in the document. Keep in mind that the language and images used in a document may reflect the historical context of the time in which it was created.

Historical Context:

Throughout United States history, individuals have taken actions to address political, economic, and social issues facing the nation. Their actions have had an impact on the United States and on American society. Three of these individuals include ***Jane Addams, Eleanor Roosevelt,*** and ***Thurgood Marshall.***

Task: Using information from the documents and your knowledge of United States history, answer the questions that follow each document in Part A. Your answers to the questions will help you write the Part B essay in which you will be asked to

Select *two* individuals mentioned in the historical context and for *each*
• Describe the conditions that led the individual to take action
• Discuss the impact of the individual's action on the United States and/or on American society

Part A
Short-Answer Questions

Directions: Analyze the documents and answer the short-answer questions that follow each document in the space provided.

Document 1

... America's settlement house movement was born in the late 19th century. The Industrial Revolution; dramatic advances in technology, transportation, and communication; and an influx in immigrants caused significant population swells in urban areas. City slums emerged where families lived in crowded, unsanitary housing. Health care was nonexistent; disease was rampant. There were few schools, and children were sent to work in factories....
  In addition, the movement focused on reform through social justice. Settlement workers and other neighbors were pioneers in the fight against racial discrimination. Their advocacy efforts also contributed to progressive legislation on housing, child labor, work conditions, and health and sanitation....

Source: "History of the Settlement House Movement," Alliance for Strong Families and Communities

1. Based on this document, state *one* condition that led to the settlement house movement. [1]

_____

_____

Document 2a

... It is easy for even the most conscientious citizen of Chicago to forget the foul smells of the stockyards and the garbage dumps, when he is living so far from them that he is only occasionally made conscious of their existence but the residents of a Settlement are perforce [of necessity] constantly surrounded by them. During our first three years on Halsted Street, we had established a small incinerator [garbage burner] at Hull-House and we had many times reported the untoward [difficult] conditions of the ward to the City Hall. We had also arranged many talks for the immigrants, pointing out that although a woman may sweep her own doorway in her native village and allow the refuse to innocently decay in the open air and sunshine, in a crowded city quarter, if the garbage is not properly collected and destroyed, a tenement-house mother may see her children sicken and die, and that the immigrants must therefore, not only keep their own houses clean, but must also help the authorities to keep the city clean....

Source: Jane Addams, *Twenty Years at Hull-House*, University of Illinois Press

Document 2b   **Hull-House Firsts**

- First Social Settlement in Chicago
- Established first public playground in Chicago
- Established first citizenship preparation classes in the United States
- Established first college extension courses in Chicago
- Initiated investigations for the first time in Chicago of truancy, typhoid fever, cocaine, children's reading, newsboys, sanitation, tuberculosis, midwifery, infant mortality, social value of the saloon
- Initiated investigations that led to creation and enactment of first factory laws in Illinois
- Initiated investigations that led to creation of first model tenement code
- First Illinois factory inspector: Hull-House resident Florence Kelley

Source: Jean Bethke Elshtain, *Jane Addams and the Dream of American Democracy: A Life*, Basic Books, 2002 (adapted)

2. Based on these documents, state *two* ways Hull-House attempted to improve conditions in Chicago. [2]

(1) _____

_____

_____

(2) _____

_____

_____

Document 3

On the 150th anniversary of Jane Addams's birth, Louise Knight wrote a book celebrating Addams's reform spirit. Knight states in the book's preface:

> ... This book is the story of how Jane Addams (1860-1935) did just that—how she increasingly thought for herself, released her own spirit, and, working with others, accomplished remarkable things. She cofounded Hull House, the nation's first settlement house (and one of the earliest community-based nonprofits) in Chicago, and in time became one of the nation's most effective reform leaders, as influential in her day on both the national and the world stages as Eleanor Roosevelt was in hers. She worked to end child labor, support unions and workers' rights, protect free speech and civil rights, respect all cultures, achieve women's suffrage and women's freedom, and promote conditions that nurtured human potential and therefore, she believed, the spread of peace. She served on the founding boards of the National Association for the Advancement of Colored People and the American Civil Liberties Union, advised every president from William McKinley to Franklin Delano Roosevelt, wrote ten books, gave hundreds of speeches, and was one of the greatest American women this nation has yet produced. Indeed, in 1912—eight years before the federal amendment giving women the vote became law—there were wistful discussions of her running for president. For the last third of her life, as founding president of the Women's International League for Peace and Freedom, she was known worldwide as an advocate for peace and women, and in 1931 she was awarded the Nobel Peace Prize....

Source: Louise W. Knight, Jane Addams: *Spirit in Action*, W. W. Norton & Company, 2010

3. According to Louise W. Knight, what is *one* impact of the work of Jane Addams? [1] _____

Document 4

> ... Unfortunately, the effects of segregation in education have not been isolated for study by social scientists. They have dealt with the whole problem of segregation, discrimination and prejudice, and although no social scientist can say that segregated schools alone give the Negro [African American] feelings of insecurity, self-hate, undermine his ego, make him feel inferior and warp his outlook on life, yet for the child the school provides the most important contact with organized society. What he learns, feels, and how he is affected there is apt to determine the type of adult he will become. Social scientists have found that children at a very early age are affected by and react to discrimination and prejudices. Thus they have agreed that it is sound to conclude that segregated schools, perhaps more than any other single factor, are of major concern to the individual of public school age and contributes greatly to the unwholesomeness and unhappy development of the personality of Negroes which the color caste system in the United States has produced....

Source: Mark V. Tushnet, ed., *Thurgood Marshall: His Speeches, Writings, Arguments, Opinions, and Reminiscences*, Lawrence Hill Books, 2001

4. According to Thurgood Marshall, what is *one* effect of segregated schools on African Americans? [1] _____

Document 5

...Early in her [Eleanor Roosevelt] husband's first term, it became clear that this was a new kind of first lady—because she was reinventing herself. As a host of urgent issues came to her attention, she quickly discovered that she had new power. Far from being a prisoner in the White House, pouring tea for ambassadors, Eleanor seemed to be everywhere at once. Just by going to a place or investigating an issue she could bring it into the full glare of nationwide publicity. She toured Washington's back alleys to publicize the conditions of the slums. Realizing that New Deal programs were geared toward men, she fought for the "forgotten woman"; she worked with Harry Hopkins to set up the women's division of the Civil Works Administration, providing, by the end of 1933, CWA jobs for 100,000 women. When she heard that farmers were slaughtering piglets, she intervened with the AAA (Agricultural Adjustment Act) administrator to ask that surplus food be given to the hungry; she lectured and wrote articles; she helped start a CCC-type camp for young jobless women; she gave a civics course at the New York Junior League; and she continually—and effectively—prodded her husband to appoint women to high government jobs....

Source: Source: James MacGregor Burns and Susan Dunn, *The Three Roosevelts: Patrician Leaders Who Transformed America*, Atlantic Monthly Press, 2001

5. According to James MacGregor Burns and Susan Dunn, state *one* way Eleanor Roosevelt attempted to improve conditions in society. [1]

_____

_____

Document 6

...The scope of Marshall's achievement in American law, however, was wider than the black American civil rights movement. His every argument spoke to individual rights for all. Protections for black Americans or any other minority, in Marshall's vision, were a function of the inviolable [untouchable] constitutional principle of individuals. When Marshall spoke about the nation's future, he projected that when the law put blacks and whites on equal footing, racial discrimination would be submerged in a greater sea of protections for individuals. As Marshall once said, black Americans are not members of the Negro [African American] race but individuals in the human race....

On cases dealing with school desegregation and affirmative action, Justice Marshall also cast his opinions as statements of individual rights, not simply as a class action for all black people. For example, his support of busing to integrate schools, even across jurisdictional boundaries, was based on the need to protect the rights of individual children who were being denied access to the best schools. And he viewed affirmative action as a matter of individual rights for black Americans, victims of discrimination who needed remedial action to be made whole....

Source: Juan Williams, *Thurgood Marshall: American Revolutionary,* Random House, 1998

6. According to Juan Williams, what was *one* way Thurgood Marshall supported individual rights for all? [1]

_____

_____

Document 7

... Eleanor Roosevelt's stand on civil rights, her insistence that America could not fight racism abroad while tolerating it at home, remains one of the affirming moments in the history of the home front during the war. Though she was naive about many aspects of the racial problem, she was far ahead of the president and the times in her understanding that separate but equal facilities were not enough, that the fact of segregation itself impaired the lives of the Negro [African American] population....

More than anyone else in the White House, Eleanor was responsible, through her relentless pressure of War Department officials, for the issuance of the two directives that forbade the designation of recreational areas by race and made government-owned and -operated buses available to every soldier regardless of race. By the end of the war, only one major step was needed to ensure true equality for Negro soldiers, and that step would come in 1948, when President Truman issued Executive Order 9981, ending segregation in the armed forces....

Source: Doris Kearns Goodwin, *No Ordinary Time,
Franklin and Eleanor Roosevelt: The Home Front in World War II*,
Simon & Schuster, 1994

7a. According to Doris Kearns Goodwin, state *one* condition that led Eleanor Roosevelt to take action on civil rights. [1]

_____

_____

7b. According to Doris Kearns Goodwin, state *one* impact Eleanor Roosevelt had on civil rights. [1]

_____

_____

Document 8a

...Convinced that America had been "spared for a purpose" from the destruction that the war inflicted on other nations, ER [Eleanor Roosevelt] seized all avenues at her disposal—columns, speeches, articles, private conversation, radio broadcasts, newsreels, and correspondence—to urge Americans to recognize what was at stake and to assume both the responsibility and the financial cost of world leadership. Fervently, she repeated that Americans must learn that "you cannot live for yourselves alone. You depend on the rest of the world and the rest of the world depends on you." UN debates on the refugee crisis, the Geneva Conventions, atomic energy, arms control, the proposed UN peace force, the creation of Israel, the implementation of apartheid, the demise of colonialism, and women's rights underscored to ER the crying need for America to accept its connection with the rest of the world—and how crucial a commonly shared vision could be in overcoming the haunting legacy of war....

Source: Allida Black, Introduction to *Tomorrow is Now*, by Eleanor Roosevelt, Penguin Books, 2012 (adapted)

8*a*. Based on this document, state *one* reason Eleanor Roosevelt urged Americans to accept the role of world leadership. [1]

Document 8b

Eleanor Roosevelt chaired the United Nations Human Rights Commission and was an important influence in the creation of the Universal Declaration of Human Rights.

Source: Joseph P. Lash, *"Life Was Meant to Be Lived": A Centenary Portrait of Eleanor Roosevelt*, W. W. Norton & Company, 1984)

8*b*. Based on this document, state *one* action Eleanor Roosevelt took to advance the cause of universal human rights. [1]

Document 9a

This is an excerpt from Thurgood Marshall's argument in the United States Supreme Court case *Brown v. Board of Education.*

> ... Those same kids in Virginia and South Carolina—and I have seen them do it—they play in the streets together, they play on their farms together, they go down the road together, they separate to go to school, they come out of school and play ball together. They have to be separated in school....
>
> They can't take race out of this case. From the day this case was filed until this moment, nobody has in any form or fashion, despite the fact I made it clear in the opening argument that I was relying on it, done anything to distinguish this statute from the Black Codes, which they must admit, because nobody can dispute, say anything anybody wants to say, one way or the other, the Fourteenth Amendment was intended to deprive the states of power to enforce Black Codes or anything else like it....
>
> The only thing can be is an inherent determination that the people who were formerly in slavery, regardless of anything else, shall be kept as near that stage as is possible, and now is the time, we submit, that this Court should make it clear that that is not what our Constitution stands for....

Source: Josh Gottheimer, ed., *Ripples of Hope: Great American Civil Rights Speeches,* Basic Civitas Books, 2003

9a. Based on this document, state *one* reason Thurgood Marshall opposed segregated schools. [1]

_____

_____

Document 9b

In *Brown v. Board of Education* the Supreme Court ruled that school desegregation should proceed "with all deliberate speed."

George E. C. Hayes, Thurgood Marshall, and James M. Nabrit Jr. are pictured congratulating each other in front of the Supreme Court on May 17, 1954, after hearing the Court's unanimous decision in the Brown case.

Source: Library of Congress (adapted)

Source: *Baltimore Afro-American,* July 2, 1955

9b. Based on this document, state *one* reason Thurgood Marshall opposed segregated schools. [1]

_____

_____

Part B
Essay

Directions: Write a well-organized essay that includes an introduction, several paragraphs, and a conclusion. Use evidence from *at least four* documents in the body of the essay. Support your response with relevant facts, examples, and details. Include additional outside information.

Historical Context:

> Throughout United States history, individuals have taken actions to address political, economic, and social issues facing the nation. Their actions have had an impact on the United States and on American society. Three of these individuals included *Jane Addams, Eleanor Roosevelt,* and *Thurgood Marshall.*

Task: Using information from the documents and your knowledge of United States history, write an essay in which you

> Choose *two* individuals mentioned in the historical context and for *each*
> • Describe the conditions that led the individual to take action
> • Discuss the impact of the individual's action on the United States and/or on American society

Guidelines:

In your essay, be sure to
- Develop all aspects of the task
- For *each* individual, describe *at least two* conditions that led that individual to take action.
- Incorporate information from *at least four* documents
- Incorporate relevant outside information
- Support the theme with relevant facts, examples, and details
- Use a logical and clear plan of organization, including an introduction and a conclusion that are beyond a restatement of the theme